HELLO WEB APP

Intro to web app development using
Python and Django.

by Tracy Osborn

Hello Web App
http://hellowebapp.com

ISBN 978-0-9863659-1-1

San Jose, California
http://limedaring.com

Revised Edition (1.1)
Printed in PRC

For my family:

*Andrey, who is the best supporpoise
anyone could ask for.*

*Westley, the 25lb biggest, baddest,
most lovable cat.*

*Molly, who is the only kind of dog I'd ever
want, except she peed on the bed last night.
Dammit.*

TABLE OF CONTENTS

118 CHAPTER 17
Moving Forward

INTRODUCTION

Have you ever wanted to build something from scratch that other people could use? You could learn carpentry, knitting, or other physical crafts—but what about something for the web?

There are tons of tutorials and instructions for writing your first website using HTML and CSS, but building something that interacts with the user—a full, complete web application—might feel unachievable and out of reach.

The reality is that starting to build a web app is not as hard as you might think. Of course it's not easy, but today's tools can help a novice web developer create a basic web app in no time at all. It's only a matter of learning the basics and launching something real, and you'll be ready (and hopefully excited) to learn more.

I used to be a web designer with no appreciable programming experience. In fact, once upon a time, I did take some introductory computer science classes at my university. After a couple of semesters, I thought I hated programming (and especially with Java), which drove me to switch my field of study to Art. I vowed to never program again.

Fast forward again to when I was working as a web designer: I kept wishing certain web apps existed. I'm sure you know the feeling. Still convinced I hated programming, I tried finding a "technical cofounder" to help me launch an idea for a web app I had. It didn't work. I was back to where I started: an idea, no cofounder. I had two options: quit or finally try to write code again.

Friends introduced me to Python, a programming language that made way more sense to me than Java, and is simply nicer looking as well; and Django, a framework built on Python to help jumpstart the creation of web apps.

Slowly but surely, I built my startup, WeddingLovely. Over the next six years, I joined the startup accelerator 500 Startups and was accepted into the Designer Fund, raised money, and eventually made WeddingLovely into a mostly-bootstrapped profitable business.

It wasn't easy. The tutorials I found online all assumed previous programming knowledge. Crazy acronyms (like MVC) abounded, explanations only further confused me, and tutorials heavily relied on the command line, a tool friendly only to experienced programmers. As a web designer the results didn't feel "real" to me until I saw them on a website.

Hello Web App is what I wished had existed when I was learning to develop web apps. I wrote this book to be free of confusing explanations and unnecessary acronyms. I talk plainly, not academically, as if we're having a conversation between friends. This book doesn't teach "best practices"—it teaches the easiest way to launch a web app.

I hope you enjoy!

1 | CHAPTER 1
WHAT WE'RE BUILDING

PYTHON IS A BEAUTIFUL PROGRAMMING LANGUAGE. As a designer, I find the clean code and organization very appealing.

Django is a Python framework (like *Ruby on Rails* is for *Ruby*, another programming language you might have heard of). It is the most feature-complete and beginner-friendly programming framework for Python: lots of useful utilities are built in and there is a massive amount of resources (tutorials as well as plugins) due to the size of the Django community.

But what exactly are we building?

Most tutorials start with a specific project. The official Django tutorial, for example, creates a polling app. But what if that tutorial subject doesn't interest you?

If you're like me, you would finish the tutorial but not feel any "ownership" over what you built because you essentially replicated another project. It's hard to relate and really understand what you're doing unless you feel involved. To that end, we're going to try something a little different here.

Hello Web App is going to walk you through building a generic "collection of things." However, this framework covers many different types of web apps you could build:

- A blog, which is a collection of posts.

- An online store, which is a collection of items to buy.

- An online directory, which is a collection of profiles.

- ... and so on and so forth.

What's written here is going to be generic and vanilla, and it's up to you to decide what exactly you're going to build using this tutorial. Pretty much the only thing you're going to change are the names of code bits, but the functionality will remain the same.

Some specific examples of what you could build using this book:

- A ratings website. Really love backpacking? You could create a website that shows your reviews for various pieces of equipment.

- A directory of people. This was my original project—I built a listing of custom wedding invitation designers. You could also do a listing of conference attendees, a list of awesome web people, such and so forth.

- An online store. There are a lot of solutions out there that help you set up a store without coding it, but it might be fun to build a store from the ground up to sell products.

- Or a blog, as mentioned above.

Take five minutes and think about a collection of objects that you're going to build using *Hello Web App*. Don't worry about scope just yet (we're getting to that); just find something you would be interested in working on.

What's your "collection of things" project?

MVP: Minimum Viable Product

Oh goodness, there's an acronym sneaking in, and I said I wouldn't do that.

Your MVP—Minimum Viable Product, a popular term in startup land—is the minimum you need to build for your app to work and be useful to users.

Sometimes people get an idea for something they want to build and spend four years trying to perfect it. But there will always be another feature to add, another bug to fix, another thing to improve, all while you could be getting real people to use your app and give you feedback (**real** feedback) on how to improve.

Building your idea might seem really intimidating, especially when working with real customers. But having real customers will be an incredible motivation to work on your web app more.

For example, my first programming project mentioned before —today, it's chock full of features. There are free and paid accounts, using Stripe and PayPal to trigger recurring charges. There are a bunch of different ways to browse pages, such as by location, by budget, or by style. There's an API so other websites can integrate vendor listings into their websites powered by my app.

None of these features existed in the first version I built.

The only real features I needed for that first version were:

- A homepage.

- A profile page for each vendor in the directory.

- A basic search by location page.

- A form so a vendor could apply to join the directory.

- ...and static pages: About, Contact, etc.

It took me only six weeks from deciding to learn how to program to launch my first app. Two weeks later, it was profiled in a prominent design blog. Swamped by customers, my startup was born.

Even the simplest of web apps can grow into something big. Something you build now could become a business.

Take some time to write down your "collection of things" project idea, and then write down every awesome feature you think it should have. Then, circle only the ones that are really truly necessary. Make your web app as small and easy to launch as possible. With luck, the lessons of *Hello Web App* will be all you need to launch your app, and if not, you'll have only a few new concepts to learn before you can launch.

2 | CHAPTER 2
PREREQUISITES

HTML and CSS

THIS TUTORIAL WORKS BEST for those who have a solid understanding of HTML and CSS.

If you haven't worked with HTML before, there are tons of resources to help get you started with front-end development. Here are a few recommended resources:

- *HTML and CSS: Design and Build Websites* (http://hellowebapp.com/1)

- *Learn to Code HTML & CSS* (http://hellowebapp.com/2)

- *Don't Fear the Internet: Basic HTML & CSS for Non-Web Designers* (http://hellowebapp.com/3)

It is recommended and highly encouraged to be comfortable building a website using basic HTML and CSS before jumping into this book. If you're not, it won't take long to get there.

Python (just a bit)

Here's the big one!

"But this is a book on how to learn how to program. Why do I need Python knowledge?" you might be asking.

The best resources for learning the basic principles in Python have already been written and are online for free—no need for this book to reinvent the wheel.

My personal favorite is *Learn Python The Hard Way* (http://hellowebapp.com/4) by Zed Shaw, which contains a series of easy and well written Python exercises. Try to get through at least half. It shouldn't take very long.

Alternatively (or in addition), the video tutorial *Hands-On Intro to Python for Beginning Programmers* (http://hellowebapp. com/5) by Jessica McKellar is excellent.

Make sure you at least partially understand the following concepts (More info: http://hellowebapp.com/6):

- Variables
- If-statements
- For-loops
- Comments

If you don't feel like an expert, or even an intermediate, that's okay—these concepts will make more and more sense to you as you play around with programming. Once you feel like you have a basic grasp, we can start building our web app.

Oh, and we're using Python 2.7. Python 3 is out, but not a lot of beginner-friendly plugins have been ported over. Python 2.7 is still *very* widely used so we're sticking with that for now.

Suggestion: A Linux or Mac computer

Unfortunately, the Windows environment doesn't play as nicely with development and programming as Unix-based systems do (such as Linux and Mac operating systems.)

This doesn't mean you can't develop on Windows, and all *Hello Web App* instructions are written with both in mind. However, in general, life will be a lot easier on a Unix-based system, so if you have the option to use something other than a Windows environment, it's highly encouraged that you do so.

If you're using Windows and have any issues with *Hello Web App*'s instructions while going through this book, check out our Windows resource page here: http://hellowebapp.com/7

3 | CHAPTER 3
GETTING STARTED

WRITING HTML AND VIEWING YOUR RESULTS right away is easy: Just point your browser to your HTML (*.html*) file and voilà—your website gets displayed!

Not so with your Python (*.py*) files—your browser has no clue what to do with Python code. To start creating web apps in Django, we first need to install Python and Django on your computer (as well as a few other useful utilities, including a local web server that will interpret your Python code and deliver responses that your web browser can understand.)

This is the most complicated part of the process. Because the instructions for installing and setting up Python keep changing over time, they live online.

Hello Web App's Python and Django installation instructions can be found here: http://hellowebapp.com/8

Once you've finished, head back to your command line (make sure you're in your virtual environment and you're in the same directory as *manage.py*) and run `python manage.py runserver`.

If everything worked correctly, you should see the Django congratuations page (congratulations!)

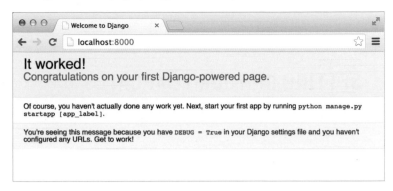

What you should see if you correctly installed Python and Django and started the local web server.

As you go through the rest of the book, keep in mind that if you ever need to check that you have the correct code snippets copied into your app, all code in the book can be found on our GitHub code repository (change chapters by clicking the "branch" button): http://hellowebapp.com/9

We also have an online forum to discuss the book and resolve issues here: http://hellowebapp.com/10

Any other information (including installation instructions, tips, and resources) can be found on our main repository here: http://hellowebapp.com/11

Now get started building your app!

CHAPTER 4
SETTING UP YOUR TEMPLATES

CONGRATS, YOU'VE LAUNCHED YOUR DJANGO WEB APP! How do
you actually make this look like a website? Note that the installation instructions didn't mention anything about templates,
HTML, CSS, or any other files. Let's set that stuff up now.

Head back to your command line, and cd into your collection
folder (the one with *models.py*). Using mkdir, create a "templates" directory, and then create *index.html* within it.

```
$ cd collection
collection $ mkdir templates
collection $ cd templates
collection/templates $ touch index.html
```

Open up *index.html* in your preferred code editor and add the
necessary pieces to display a typical webpage. We're going to use
HTML5 but only the bare bones for now—we can get fancy later.

index.html
```
<!doctype html>
<html>
<head>
```

```
    <title>My Hello Web App Project</title>
</head>
<body>
    <h1>Hello World!</h1>
    <p>I am a basic website.</p>
</body>
</html>
```

If you open up your browser and go to *http://localhost:8000*, you'll still see the same default page you saw before—none of the HTML above. We need to tell Django how to get to that file.

Adding a URL to urls.py

Django doesn't know what to do with the *index.html* file we just created. So head to *urls.py*, which is in the same folder as *settings.py*—we're going to associate the root directory (*/*) with the newly created *index.html*.

In *urls.py*'s entries area, find the `urlpatterns` line, remove the pre-existing comments, and add in the lines indicated:

urls.py
```
from django.conf.urls import patterns, url
from django.contrib import admin
from collection import views

urlpatterns = [
    url(r'^$', views.index, name='home'),
    url(r'^admin/', include(admin.site.urls)),
]
```

There are essentially four parts to this new line:

• `url()` encases the entry to indicate it's a URL entry.

- `r'^$'` is the beginning of the URL pattern. Might look confusing, but just remember the pattern for now.

- `views.index` means that we'll use the index view in *views.py* in our app `collection` (imported at the top). We'll create this soon.

- Last, `name='home'` is optional, but allows us to assign a name to this URL so we can refer to it in the future as "home". I'll explain how this ties in later.

I am using the "typical" *urls.py* layout here, but if it's more understandable to you, you can layout the URL definition like this:

urls.py
```
urlpatterns = [
    url(
        regex=r'^$',
        view=views.index,
        name='home',
    ),
    url(r'^admin/', include(admin.site.urls)),
]
```

This will help you keep track of which bit is what. I'm going to keep using the previous configuration in this book though, since it's how it's usually laid out in Django.

Apologies if URL configuration sounds complicated. The most you need to remember here is that there is a regular expression for the path, then the view definition, and then we gave the URL a name. We can easily copy and paste from this template in the future for new URL entries.

Creating your first view

Now that we have a template and a URL entry, we need to tie them together, so that the URL will display the template. This is *views.py*'s job, which lives in the `collection` app.

There are a ton of different ways to display a template simply in the views, and my favorite is Django's shortcut function called `render`. This is something you'll need to import, but Django anticipates that you'll use it and already has it added to the top of *views.py* for us.

views.py

```
from django.shortcuts import render

# Create your views here.
def index(request):
    # this is your new view
    return render(request, 'index.html')
```

Basically, *urls.py* will catch that someone wants the homepage and points to this piece of code, which will render the *index. html* template. Now open up your browser and check out the new homepage on *http://localhost:8000*. Woohoo!

Adding static files

We're now displaying the HTML file we created, but how do we get CSS styling in there? Unfortunately it's not as simple as creating a CSS directory and linking the stylesheets in our HTML file.

Let's go ahead and create the directory for static files now, which Django uses for files like style sheets. In your app (remember we named it collection—the folder that contains *models.py*), create a "static" directory, and within it, add in directories for CSS, Javascript, and images. In the CSS directory, add a blank *style.css* file.

```
$ cd collection
collection $ mkdir static
collection $ cd static
collection/static $ mkdir images
collection/static $ mkdir js
collection/static $ mkdir css
collection/static $ cd css
collection/static/css $ touch style.css
```

Head back into your *index.html* page. We'll need to tell Django that there are static files used on this page, so at the top (like imports in *views.py* and *urls.py*) add {% load staticfiles %}. Why the {%? We'll get to that soon.

Now that we can add static files to this template, add your CSS tag to the <HEAD> just like this:

index.html
```
{% load staticfiles %}
<!doctype html>
<html>
<head>
    <title>My Hello Web App Project</title>
```

```
    <link rel="stylesheet" href="{% static 'css/style.css' %}" />
</head>
<body>
    <h1>Hello World!</h1>
    <p>I am a basic website.</p>
</body>
</html>
```

We want to avoid using relative paths, such as href="../css/
style.css". For optimization purposes, someday later you
might want to move the static files of your project to a different
server (such as Amazon's *Simple Storage Service*, or S3), and by
avoiding relative paths with Django's static files URL utility, your
CSS path will always use what's defined in your settings and will
magically work even if you change your static file's locations.

At this point, feel free to add some stylesheet declarations to
your *style.css* file and check out *http://localhost:8000* again (run
`python manage.py runserver` in your command line again if
you need to do so).

style.css
```
body {
    background-color: cornflowerblue;
}
```

Nice! Feel free to update your CSS more at this point.

To link to any static file from a template, use the `{% static 'FILELOCATION/FILENAME.TYPE' %}` syntax, such as `{% static 'js/script.js' %}` or `{% static 'images/logo.jpg' %}`. Keep in mind you still need the IMG HTML tag when displaying images, for example: `<img src="{% static 'images/logo.jpg' %}" alt=""/>`

All that said, don't worry about this within your CSS files—feel free to use relative paths because your static files should always be together anyways.

```
h1 {
    /* for example... */
    background-image: url(../images/logo.png);
}
```

Now you can add static files and style your website! Don't forget to commit your work with git (review git on our git tips page here: http://hellowebapp.com/12).

Next up, Django has a bunch of awesome template utilities that'll elevate these static HTML files and make them a lot more interesting (and fun to work with).

5 | FUN WITH TEMPLATE TAGS

BEFORE WE GET INTO DYNAMIC DATA, let's explore the fun things that Django's template system has built in.

Building complex templates with inheritance

One of the biggest advantages of using a framework like Django is template inheritance. Instead of having a bunch of files that repeat information (such as `<header>...</header>` tags, your nav, etc.), you can have one base layout template that all other templates import.

In your templates directory, add a new file called *base.html*.

```
$ cd collection/templates
collection/templates $ touch base.html
```

We're going to strip out all website-common code from *index.html* and stick it into *base.html*:

base.html
```
{% load staticfiles %}
<!doctype html>
```

```
<html>
<head>
    <title><!-- we want to override page titles --></title>
    <link rel="stylesheet" href="{% static 'css/style.css' %}" />
</head>
<body>
    <!-- as well as override content bits -->
</body>
</html>
```

We can define blocks in our layout template where information can be added or overwritten. For example, we'll add {% block content %}{% endblock content %} where we'd like the body content from *index.html* to go. We can also add other overridable blocks in our layout template: I usually add a block for the page title, optional header information (for including other CSS files, for example), and right-before-closing-body tag (for adding other Javascript files).

base.html now:

```
{% load staticfiles %}
<!doctype html>
<html>
<head>
    <title>
        {% block title %}
            My Hello Web App Project
        {% endblock title %}
    </title>
    <link rel="stylesheet" href="{% static 'css/style.css' %}" />
    {% block header %}{% endblock header %}
</head>
<body>
    {% block content %}{% endblock content %}
    {% block footer %}{% endblock footer %}
</body>
</html>
```

Note that we have content in the {% block title %} tags. That will be our default content that'll show if child pages don't override the title.

Head back over to *index.html*, and delete everything other than our content that we removed from the new layout template. To indicate that this template has a layout template that will extend, we'll add {% extends 'base.html' %} to the top of the template, and then we can add in blocks in the template for the sections we defined in our *base.html* template.

Our new *index.html*:

```
{% extends 'base.html' %}
{% block title %}
    Homepage - {{ block.super }}
{% endblock title %}

{% block content %}
    <h1>Hello World!</h1>
    <p>I am a basic website.</p>
{% endblock content %}
```

A few important things to note:

- Each block (like {% block content %}) has the name we defined in our *base.html* file so the template engine knows where to render which part.

- Check out the title block. See the {{ block.super }}? In our *base.html* file, we defined "My Hello Web App Project" as the default content. {{ block.super }} will insert the contents of the default block instead of overriding it. Now our page titles can have both the local page name as well as the title of the website. If you ever change the main title of the website, you only have to update it in *base.html* and it will automatically update the child pages.

- If you're loading static assets like images, you'll still need to add `{% load staticfiles %}` to the top of the base layout file. We're not loading static files in *index.html* so we haven't added this loading tag, but keep in mind if you add static files to your version.

Now you can add new simple pages to your website without having to repeat the same code over and over!

Adding a few other static pages

Having template inheritance doesn't feel real until you have multiple templates all extending one layout template.

Let's create a few extra pages: an *about.html* and *contact.html*. First, create the HTML files in your templates directory. I'm going to make it easy by copying our *index.html* file because it already has the `{% block %}` tags added for inheritance.

```
templates $ cp index.html about.html
templates $ cp index.html contact.html
```

Then open the pages and edit the HTML so it makes sense for each page:

about.html
```
{% extends 'base.html' %}
{% block title %}
    About - {{ block.super }}
{% endblock title %}

{% block content %}
    <h1>About page</h1>
    <p>About content.</p>
{% endblock content %}
```

contact.html
```
{% extends 'base.html' %}
{% block title %}
    Contact - {{ block.super }}
{% endblock title %}

{% block content %}
    <h1>Contact page</h1>
    <p>Contact content.</p>
{% endblock content %}
```

Last, we'll need to create a few new URL definitions in *urls.py*. If your new template won't display information from your data-base—only simple HTML and CSS—then we can simplify our URL definition with a shortcut without having to add anything to *views.py*.

Open your *urls.py*—we're going to import something new and add the new URL definitions:

urls.py
```
from django.conf.urls import include, url
from django.contrib import admin
from django.views.generic import TemplateView
from collection import views

urlpatterns = [
    url(r'^$', views.index, name='home'),
    url(r'^about/$',
        TemplateView.as_view(template_name='about.html'),
        name='about'),
    url(r'^contact/$',
        TemplateView.as_view(template_name='contact.html'),
        name='contact'),
    url(r'^admin/', include(admin.site.urls)),
]
```

These new patterns are nearly the same thing we had before when we made a URL entry: The regular expression at the beginning and the name of the view at the end. Instead of pointing to a function in *views.py* though, we're going to use Django's *generic view* called `TemplateView` that basically says, "Hey, just display this template."

Add navigation

Every page will need to have navigation, so we'll add that to our layout template. Open it and add the following basic HTML (I also added a header and some other bits):

base.html

```
{% load staticfiles %}
<!doctype html>
<html>
<head>
    <title>
        {% block title %}
            My Hello Web App Project
        {% endblock title %}
    </title>
    <link rel="stylesheet" href="{% static 'css/style.css' %}" />
    {% block header %}{% endblock header %}
</head>
<body>
    <header>
        <h1>Hello Web App</h1>
        <nav>
            <ul>
                <li><a href="{% url 'home' %}">Home</a></li>
                <li><a href="{% url 'about' %}">About</a></li>
                <li><a href="{% url 'contact' %}">Contact</a></li>
            </ul>
        </nav>
    </header>
```

```
    {% block content %}{% endblock content %}
    {% block footer %}{% endblock footer %}
</body>
</html>
```

Surprise: We're not going to link to other HTML files like we
normally would. This is why we name URLs—we can tell
Django that we want to link to the URL named "home," and
Django will automatically insert the right path. In the future,
if you ever decide to change the URL (like changing *about*/ to /
about-us/), you would just need to change it in your *urls.py* file
and Django will update your templates for you.

Check out your website with it's shiny, new navigation:

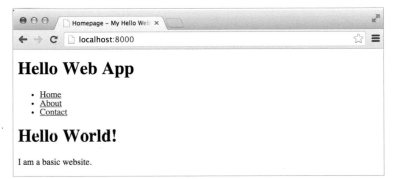

Passing in variables and template tags

At this point you could launch this basic website, but dynamic
content is really why we're here.

To show how variables get passed into the templates from the
view, head back to *views.py* to the index function (a function is
what each of the code blocks starting with def is). For fun, let's
define a variable with an integer and pass it to the view to see
the fun things that Django's template tags can do.

We're going to create a variable that holds a number and then make this variable available to the template. Update your view to the following:

views.py
```python
def index(request):
    # defining the variable
    number = 6
    # passing the variable to the view
    return render(request, 'index.html', {
        'number': number,
    })
```

Back over in *index.html*, we can access these variables in two ways:

- `{{ variable }}`: Surrounded by two curly braces, this simply displays what was passed in.

- `{% tag %}`: `{% %}` is django's version of `<  >` in HTML. A tag in curly braces/percent signs means we're doing something either with that variable or to the template, such as loading static files.

To see this in action, let's first display the variable. Add this to your *index.html* file:

index.html
```html
{% extends 'base.html' %}
{% block title %}
    Homepage - {{ block.super }}
{% endblock title %}

{% block content %}
    <h1>Hello World!</h1>
    <!-- here's the variable we are passing in -->
    <p>{{ number }}</p>
{% endblock content %}
```

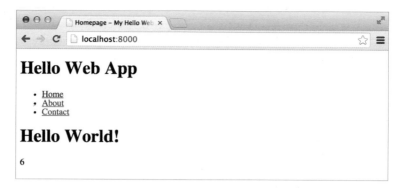

Ta-da! Django translates `{{ number }}` to the value of the variable called number from the view which was passed into the template.

Django also allows you to use logic similar to Python within the templates—most importantly, *if-else statements* and *for loops*. (Can't remember what these are? Refer to *Learn Python The Hard Way* (http://hellowebapp.com/13) for a refresher.)

Check out an *if-else statement* in action:

```
<p>{% if number %}Number exists!{% endif %}</p>
```

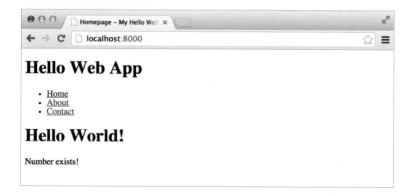

And another example:

```
<p>There are six dogs! <b>
{% if number == 6 %}
    True
{% else %}
    False
{% endif %}
</b></p>
```

Django also has a lot of fun template tags (http://hellowebapp.com/14). For example, if you were passing in the number of dogs in your website, you could make a word plural if the number is more than one.

```
<p>There are {{ number }} dog{{ number|pluralize }}!</p>
```

This template tag also accepts different suffixes:

```
<p>There are {{ number }} walrus{{ number|pluralize:"es" }}!</p>
```

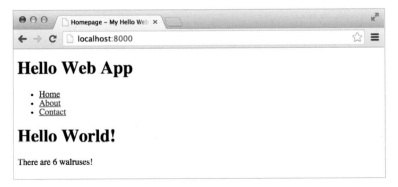

Django has an optional library you can use to format and "humanize" numbers. Add `'django.contrib.humanize'`, to your INSTALLED_APPS list in *settings.py*:

```
INSTALLED_APPS = (
    ...
    'django.contrib.staticfiles',
    'django.contrib.humanize',
)
```

Then add `{% load humanize %}` to the top of our template. We're going to start with apnumber, which spells out the numbers 1-9:

index.html
```
{% extends 'base.html' %}
{% load humanize %}
{% block title %}
    Homepage - {{ block.super }}
{% endblock title %}

{% block content %}
    <h1>Hello World!</h1>
```

```
<p>There are {{ number|apnumber }} dogs!</p>
{% endblock content %}
```

Note that what was displayed as "6" before is now "six". Read more about humanize and the other fun options it has here: http://hellowebapp.com/15

There are also a bunch of template tags that work on strings. Let's change our view:

views.py
```
def index(request):
    number = 6
    # don't forget the quotes because it's a string, not an integer
    thing = "Thing name"
    return render(request, 'index.html', {
        'number': number,
        # don't forget to pass it in, and the last comma
        'thing': thing,
    })
```

As well as our template:

```
<p>This is my name: {{ thing }}</p>
```

So now we can play with more fun template tags, like this one which would turn it into a slug, a shortened, lowercased version of a string used for URLs:

```
<p>This is my name: {{ thing|slugify }}</p>
```

Feel like using title case?

```
<p>This is my name: {{ thing|title }}</p>
```

Perhaps it's too long of a name for you? Truncate it:

```
<p>This is my name: {{ thing|truncatewords:1 }}</p>
```

I hope at this point you can see how Django's template system has a bunch of powerful features that knock a static website out of the water. Check out the full list of included Django template tags here: http://hellowebapp.com/14. It gets even more fun when you have real dynamic data to work with, which is coming up in the next section.

Don't forget to commit your work at this point!

6 | CHAPTER SIX
ADDING DYNAMIC DATA

NOW THAT WE KNOW WHAT WE CAN DO with templates and know how variables can be passed in from the view, we'll head back to *models.py* to actually define the dynamic information that we want to add to and store in our database—basically, the *things* in our *collection*.

Your local database

Back when we were setting up Django (the instructions that live in our GitHub online repository: http://hellowebapp. com/16), Django already created our database for us using *SQLite3*.

We're using SQLite3 on our computer because it's quick and easy, but it's not an appropriate database if you were to launch your app—it was built to support only a single user at a time. Fine for development, but research other database solutions before launching your web app. More on that later, don't worry.

Creating a superuser—you!

We're going to be using Django's super handy admin, which means we need to create an account for yourself so you can pop in any time to check out the state of your web app.

Type this into your command line:

```
$ python manage.py createsuperuser
```

This'll prompt you to create an admin user—choose any username, email address, and password that you like. It can always be changed later.

Setting up your model

Remember that this tutorial is teaching you to build a "collection of things," which is going to seem complicated now that we're in the model, where we actually define what our thing is.

Thankfully any "collection of things" generally would need the same couple of basic properties (keeping with our MVP philosophy):

- *Name* of the thing.
- *Description* of the thing.
- *Slug* of the thing, used in its future URL.

We can add a lot more info to our Thing eventually, but we're going to start with this for now, keeping everything minimal to start.

The first two attributes we're defining are fairly obvious to why we need them. We're also going to add a slug because eventually we're going to build individual pages for these objects, and it's a lot easier to have the slug for the object already defined in the database for creating URLs in the future.

URLs can't have any spaces and are best limited to letters, numbers, underscores, or hyphens—so the URL for something named "This Beautiful Something" would have a slug of this-beautiful-something. We're also going to make this field automatically fill itself out—more on that soon.

In *models.py*, we're going to build a model for the information we want to store. Here's where you're going to want to customize the titles—I'll give the generic example first, and then a customized example after to make it easy.

models.py

```
from django.db import models

class Thing(models.Model):
    name = models.CharField(max_length=255)
    description = models.TextField()
    slug = models.SlugField(unique=True)
```

If you were building a directory of invitation designers, you might want to change the class from Thing to Profile—so, class Profile(models.Model).

For a list of awesome surfboards, you could change it to Surfboard—so, class Surfboard(models.Model).

You get the drift.

As for the rest of the model, this is basically what we're defining:

- A *name* field (with a character limit of 255 characters—you're required to define a limit, and 255 is a good basic limit.)

- A *description* field with a text field (which doesn't require a limit—think of these like HTML forms, such <input>s versus <textareas>.)

- A *slug* field using Django's SlugField (http://hellowebapp. com/17) that'll add some automatic checking to make sure it's always in the right format, and ensures uniqueness against other objects because we use it in each unique object's URL.

Finishing setting up your database with migrations

Think of the database like a giant spreadsheet filled with information about our users—names, descriptions, etc. One day we decide to add another column of information for all of our users—a location. How do we fill in that column for those pre-existing users? We *could* do it by hand. What if the spreadsheet had thousands of rows? What then?

Thankfully Django comes included with a database migrations utility that both tracks changes to the database when new fields are added, edited, or removed; and gracefully updates the existing database to make sure everything plays nicely with one another.

We'll going to create our *initial migration*. This is basically the starting point to help Django track the changes you make to your database, so when you make new changes, Django will know exactly what changed and will migrate the information correctly to the new database plan (known as a schema).

We need to tell Django we're creating the initial migration, so in your command line (in the same folder as *manage.py*), type this in:

```
$ python manage.py makemigrations
```

And this is what you should see as a result:

```
Migrations for 'collection':
  0001_initial.py:
    - Create model Thing
```

We've created the migration file, but we haven't applied it. Run `python manage.py migrate` next:

```
$ python manage.py migrate
Operations to perform:
  Apply all migrations: admin, contenttypes, collection, auth,
sessions
Running migrations:
  Applying collection.0001_initial... OK
```

Like above, we're running the `migrate` command, telling Django to search for new migrations and apply them to the existing database tables.

Our database is now set up and we can start adding some information!

Using the Django admin

The other huge advantage Django has as a Python framework is the included visual administration system. This'll allow you to see and update all information stored in your database in your browser without having to log into your database using the command line.

We need to tell the admin to display the information in our `Thing` model (or whatever you called it). The admin doesn't grab info from our model automatically.

Within your `collection` app folder, open up *admin.py* and add the following lines:

admin.py

```
from django.contrib import admin

# import your model
from collection.models import Thing

# and register it
admin.site.register(Thing)
```

This is the bare minimum that you'll need to get your new model to show up in the admin. Let's add one more extra bit just to make it more awesome:

```
from django.contrib import admin

# import your model
from collection.models import Thing

# set up automated slug creation
class ThingAdmin(admin.ModelAdmin):
    model = Thing
    list_display = ('name', 'description',)
    prepopulated_fields = {'slug': ('name',)}

# and register it
admin.site.register(Thing, ThingAdmin)
```

Don't forget to add ThingAdmin to your register statement at the bottom of your file.

First, list_display tells Django that we want the name and description of our fields to show up in the admin.

We set up our model to require a slug, but we don't want to fill it out manually—much better to have it auto-created by Django magic. The ThingAdmin block basically says that we're going to use the model Thing and we're going to prepopulate

the slug field based off the name field when someone types the
name of a Thing in the admin. You'll see this in a second.

Now if you go back to your browser and go to
http://localhost:8000/admin, you can log in using the admin
username and password that you made earlier when creating
a superuser.

Voilà: a visual representation of your database information
—your admin panel.

As you can see, we have links for a User database as well as an
area for our new app (Collection) and a link for our models
defined in the app (so far, only Thing).

Click on Users and you can see the entry for your admin user account (you!), and if you click on that entry, you can update any of the information on that User account.

Here's where you can see that Django's included User accounts really saves us some time: The password on the account is hashed for us, which is kind-of like encryption but one-way and can't be reversed. This is important because if the database ever leaks, hackers won't be able to reverse our users' original passwords. This would be especially-bad because many folks use the same password on many sites. Staying up-to-date with the latest security practices is a full-time job, but Django takes care of these decisions for us. Thanks, Django!

If you back up a few screens to check out the Things area, it's empty because we haven't added any new Things to our site yet—or people, or surfboards, or whatever you decided to call your model. Let's add our first one.

Back out of the User area and click on "Things" (or whatever you named your model). At the top right of the page, there's a button to add objects to your database.

As you can see, this is a handy place for us to see, add, change, and remove any account added to our website without logging into the database through the command line. Our slug was also auto-created, saving us valuable time. Win!

Add a couple of more test objects to your database:

Customers can't see the admin though (and really shouldn't ever—this panel should only be used for administrative use).

Next up, let's get our database information showing up in the templates. Don't forget to commit your work!

CHAPTER 7
DISPLAYING DYNAMIC INFORMATION IN THE TEMPLATES

IT'S GREAT THAT WE CAN SEE our information in the admin, but now we need to be able to display that information in our templates and ergo in our website.

Querying for info from the database

Views are where all of our logic will go for displaying in the templates, so it's back to *views.py* we go.

Find the index view back from when we were playing with template tags:

views.py
```
def index(request):
    number = 6
    # don't forget the quotes because it's a string, not an integer
    thing = "Thing name"
    return render(request, 'index.html', {
        'number': number,
```

```
    # don't forget to pass it in, and the last comma
    'thing': thing,
})
```

Right now it's essentially saying: "When the index page is viewed, display this template and pass along these two variables."

Now we want to update that to "When the index page is viewed, find all things in our database, display this template, and pass those things along to that template."

Here's the new view. Don't forget, if you've renamed Thing to something else in your model, make sure to update all instances below:

views.py
```
from django.template import render
from collection.models import Thing

# the rewritten view!
def index(request):
    things = Thing.objects.all()
    return render(request, 'index.html', {
        'things': things,
    })
```

First, we need to tell the view that we need some information from the model, so we've added an import statement to the top of the page (that's the `from collection.models import Thing`).

Then in the index view, we're using *QuerySets* (more info: http://hellowebapp.com/18) to ask for all Thing objects from the database.

Head back to the template, where we were having fun with template tags before. We now are passing along a variable containing all the Things in our database, so now we need to display that in the template.

Update your *index.html*:

```
{% extends 'base.html' %}
{% block title %}
    Homepage - {{ block.super }}
{% endblock title %}

{% block content %}
    {% for thing in things %}
    <h2>{{ thing.name }}</h2>
    <p>{{ thing.description }}</p>
    {% endfor %}
{% endblock content %}
```

This is a loop that'll iterate over all the objects in the things variable, displaying the name for each Thing. Remember that {% %} shows an action and {{ }} prints out the variable.

Voilà: We're showing the information from our database in our homepage!

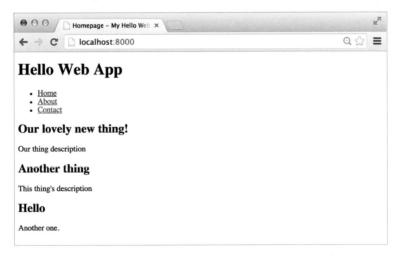

Retrieving and filtering information with QuerySets

One of the biggest things to remember about programming is that accessing the database is one of the slowest things your app can do, and can lead to a slow website if you're not careful. That means querying for all Things when you only want one Thing is inefficient. *Don't* do something like this in your template:

```
{% for thing in things %}
{% if thing.name == "Hello" %}
    {{ thing.name }}
{% endif %}
{% endfor %}
```

It would be much faster if we could just query for that one Thing instead, rather than getting all of them and then just searching for just one in the template, right?

QuerySets come with a lot of extra stuff to help filter the records in your database. For example, if you wanted the Thing named "Hello," you could do this instead:

```
# what we had before
things = Thing.objects.all()

# just getting one object!
correct_thing = Thing.objects.get(name='Hello')
```

The .get() method will retrieve the object that matches the query, but keep in mind it'll throw an error if more than one object is found (or none.) If you want to grab a bunch of things that match, you'll use .filter():

```
things = Thing.objects.filter(name='Hello')
```

So, remember: `.get()` is when you want one, exact object; `.filter()` is for when you could possibly retrieve more than one result.

When Django returns a bunch of items, we can also have it return it alphabetically using `.order_by()`:

```
things = Thing.objects.filter(name='Hello').order_by('name')
```

Another useful method is to look up whether a field contains something using `contains`:

```
things = Thing.objects.filter(name__contains='Hello')
```

Check out your website to see the update:

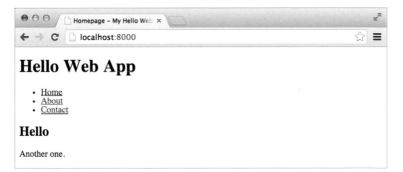

Note how `contains` gets added onto the field that we're searching on using a double-underscore (`__`). If we had just `name=`, we'd only get **exact** name matches, but `name__contains=` will get **incomplete** matches.

We can also tell it to return a random order as well using `?`:

```
things = Thing.objects.all().order_by('?')
```

This is just an overview of the basic queries we can make with Django. For more (a lot more, but it's pretty interesting), check

---

out Django's documentation of QuerySets: http://hellowebapp.com/18.

Before you forget, change the query in your view back to grabbing all objects:

views.py
```
from django.shortcuts import render
from collection.models import Thing

def index(request):
    things = Thing.objects.all()
    return render(request, 'index.html', {
        'things': things,
    })
```

Congrats—we now have objects in our database showing up on our website! Commit your work, and now let's move on to creating individual pages for these objects.

8 | CHAPTER 8
SETTING UP
INDIVIDUAL OBJECT PAGES

WE NOW HAVE A LIST OF ALL THE OBJECTS in our database on
our homepage—wouldn't it be nice for each object to have its
own page?

Adding the new pages to our URL definitions

Following our usual URLs-views-templates routine, let's
head over to the *urls.py* file to add the new URL scheme for
our new pages.

We're going to remove the commented out default stuff from
before, and add a new line:

urls.py

```
...
urlpatterns = [
    url(r'^$', views.index, name='home'),
    url(r'^about/$',
        TemplateView.as_view(template_name='about.html'),
        name='about'),
```

```
url(r'^contact/$',
    TemplateView.as_view(template_name='contact.html'),
    name='contact'),
url(r'^things/(?P<slug>[-\w]+)/$', views.thing_detail,
    name='thing_detail'),
url(r'^admin/', include(admin.site.urls)),
]
```

Whoa, holy scary regular expression, right?

To be honest, if you stopped me and asked me to write that line from scratch, I wouldn't be able to. I copy and paste it from project to project, and just update the small things that matter, leaving the regular expression ("regex") alone. Learning regex, while handy, is definitely not required for basic web app development (you can learn more here if you want, though: http://hellowebapp.com/19)

Going over the bits in the new line:

- `url(`: Beginning of the url definition.

- `r'^things/`: Basically says "starts with 'things.'" You can update this to match your model, so `r'profiles/` or `r'surfboards/` for example. r stands for "raw" and ensures the regex is executed literally.

- `(?P<slug>[-\w]+)/$`: Basically means "matches any word and call it 'slug.'" The only important part to remember is that you can change 'slug' for other uses, but for this use, we should call it slug.

- `'collection.views.thing_detail',`: We're using the soon-to-be-created `thing_detail` view.

- `, name='thing_detail'),`: And this URL is named `thing_detail`.

Create the view

Our second view, woohoo!

Back to *views.py* and add the new view in:

views.py
```python
from django.shortcuts import render
from collection.models import Thing

def index(request):
    things - Thing.objects.all()
    return render(request, 'index.html', {
        'things': things,
    })

def thing_detail(request, slug):
    # grab the object...
    thing = Thing.objects.get(slug=slug)
    # and pass to the template
    return render(request, 'things/thing_detail.html', {
        'thing': thing,
    })
```

Fairly simple. Note that at the top of the view, we now have slug passed in from *urls.py*—remember that this was what was in that big, scary regex bit.

And now to the template...

Setting up the template

We'll need to create the new HTML file that the view indicates.

```
$ cd collection/templates
collection/templates $ mkdir things
```

```
collection/templates $ cd things
collection/templates/things $ cp ../index.html thing_detail.html
```

We could write `touch thing_detail.html` to create a blank file, but to avoid writing out the content blocks and save us some typing, we'll just copy the index file.

Of course, feel free to update `thing` and `things` here to match what you're building (don't forget to update the view if you do so). We're putting the detail page under a separate folder to keep all the templates that deal with individual `things` in one place.

Here's our new individual object HTML template:

thing_detail.html
```
{% extends 'base.html' %}
{% block title %}
    {{ thing.name }} - {{ block.super }}
{% endblock title %}

{% block content %}
    <h1>{{ thing.name }}</h1>
    <p>{{ thing.description }}</p>
{% endblock content %}
```

`{{ thing }}` is the object we passed in from the database, and we can access the fields we set in the model (name and description) by adding the model field after a dot—basically, `{{ thing.name }}`.

How do we get to these individual pages? Let's update our index view to make the list of objects we're displaying to link to their individual pages.

Our new *index.html* template:

```
{% extends 'base.html' %}
{% block title %}
    Homepage - {{ block.super }}
{% endblock title %}

{% block content %}
    {% for thing in things %}
        <h2><a href="{% url 'thing_detail' slug=thing.slug %}">
            {{ thing.name }}
        </a></h2>
        <p>{{ thing.description }}</p>
    {% endfor %}
{% endblock content %}
```

We're going to use Django's named URLs again. We named our detail pages (back in *urls.py*) `thing_detail`, and we also need to pass in the slug in the named URL link so it knows which exact `thing` to make a link for.

Now we have an index page full of links:

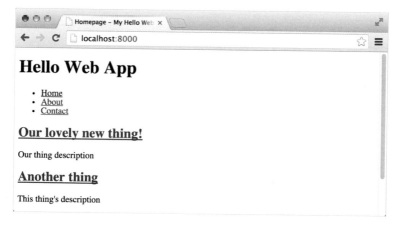

Which link to the object's respective page:

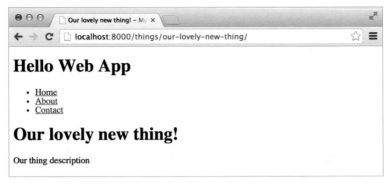

We are one step toward a working website that's useful to visitors and potential customers! Don't forget to commit your work.

CHAPTER 9
FORMS.PY FUNSIES

WE NOW HAVE A BASIC WEBSITE that showcases a collection of objects, with individual pages for each object. However at the moment, if you needed to change any data for an object (basically, changing the name or description), you can only do that through the admin. Let's start working with Django forms and create pages on the website that'll allow us to update the information for each object inside the actual website.

Update your urls.py

As usual, we'll need to do the typical create-a-URL, create-a-view, create-a-template routine we've been doing. So, head back to over to *urls.py*, and add the indicated line:

urls.py

```
. . .
urlpatterns = [
    url(r'^$', views.index, name='home'),
    url(r'^about/$',
        TemplateView.as_view(template_name='about.html'),
        name='about'),
```

```
url(r'^contact/$',
    TemplateView.as_view(template_name='contact.html'),
        name='contact'),
url(r'^things/(?P<slug>[-\w]+)/$', views.thing_detail,
        name='thing_detail'),
# new line we're adding!
url(r'^things/(?P<slug>[-\w]+)/edit/$',
    views.edit_thing, name='edit_thing'),
url(r'^admin/', include(admin.site.urls)),
]
```

Note: *We set up our models so that we're assuming one* User *to one* Thing. *In that case, we actually don't need to include the slug in the URL, so our future code could be a bit simpler. But I'm going to show you how to do it this way, because it's more flexible in case you set you web app up so* Users *can own multiple* Things.

And then add your view...

Go to your *views.py* file to add the new view. Add the below code below your `thing_detail` view (apologies, it's quite the doozy but the comments should help):

views.py
```
# add to top of the file
from django.shortcuts import render, redirect
from collection.forms import ThingForm
from collection.models import Thing


...
# add below your thing_detail view
def edit_thing(request, slug):
    # grab the object...
    thing = Thing.objects.get(slug=slug)
    # set the form we're using...
    form_class = ThingForm
```

```
# if we're coming to this view from a submitted form,
if request.method == 'POST':
    # grab the data from the submitted form
    form = form_class(data=request.POST, instance=thing)
    if form.is_valid():
        # save the new data
        form.save()
        return redirect('thing_detail', slug=thing.slug)

# otherwise just create the form
else:
    form = form_class(instance=thing)

# and render the template
return render(request, 'things/edit_thing.html', {
    'thing': thing,
    'form': form,
})
```

The most complicated view we've added yet! We've added an
if-statement, which allows the view to do two different things
depending on whether we're just displaying the form, or
dealing with the new data after the form has been submitted.
Multi-use view!

Create your forms.py file

In the view, we make reference to ThingForm, which we haven't
created yet. It's really handy to have all your form information
in one place, so we're going to add a file called *forms.py* into
our collection app:

```
$ cd collection
collection $ touch forms.py
```

Open it up and add the following code:

forms.py
```
from django.forms import ModelForm
from collection.models import Thing

class ThingForm(ModelForm):
    class Meta:
        model = Thing
        fields = ('name', 'description',)
```

A part of Django's "magic" is the ability to create forms directly from your model — thus, the *ModelForm* (More info: http://hellowebapp.com/20). We just need to tell it which model to base itself on, as well as (optionally) which fields we want it to include. This way we don't allow updating of the slug in the form because it should be set automatically from the Thing name.

So, plainly speaking: This form is based on the Thing model, and allows updating of its name and description fields.

Last, the template. Head back into your *things* folder and add a template to edit your object:

```
$ cd collection/templates/things
collection/templates/things $ touch edit_thing.html
```

In the view above, you'll see we're passing in the form. Thankfully, Django has another useful utility for displaying the form in the template. Here's what we'll add into our template:

edit_thing.html
```
{% extends 'base.html' %}
{% block title %}
    Edit {{ thing.name }} - {{ block.super }}
{% endblock title %}
```

```
{% block content %}
    <h1>Edit "{{ thing.name }}"</h1>
    <form role="form" action="" method="post">
        {% csrf_token %}
        {{ form.as_p }}
        <button type="submit">Submit</button>
    </form>
{% endblock %}
```

A couple of things to note:

- What's that whole `{% csrf_token %}` stuff? Django
  requires this added to every form that submits via POST.
  Long story short, it's *Cross Site Request Forgery* protection
  (More info: http://hellowebapp.com/21) that ships with
  Django. The website will complain if you don't have it
  because it's a security measure.

- Adding `.as_p` to our form variable is optional—it'll render
  the form fields wrapped in <p> tags. You can also do
  `.as_ul` (wrapped in <li> tags, you'll still need to add the
  surrounding <ul> tag) or as `.as_table` (you'll still need
  to add surrounding <table> tags.) Read more about that
  here: http://hellowebapp.com/22.

To make it easy to access this page, add a link to this page from
our object view:

thing_detail.html
```
{% extends 'base.html' %}
{% block title %}
    {{ thing.name }} - {{ block.super }}
{% endblock title %}

{% block content %}
    <h1>{{ thing.name }}</h1>
```

```
    <p>{{ thing.description }}</p>
    <a href="{% url 'edit_thing' slug=thing.slug %}">
        Edit me!
    </a>
{% endblock content %}
```

Head to the browser to check it out:

Neat, all of the form fields already have the current information for the object. Thanks, Django! Feel free to edit and save any information here and it'll automagically update the database, and ergo, all the information on your website.

Now we can update the information about these objects in our website, but still can only create new objects from our admin. Commit your work. Next, we'll add a registration page so customers can create pages of their own.

Note: *While your slug was created automatically based on the Name when we added the object, changing the name of the object won't change the slug. For example, if your name was "This Name" and your slug was* this-name, *and you updated the name to "Another Name", the slug will continue to be* this-name. *What's up with that? It's actually quite smart—if this page was on the Internet with people linking to it, and the slug (ergo the URL) changed, all of the links would break. Django, by default, keeps the slugs the same as when they were created to make sure all external links continue to work. You can manually override this in your admin, however.*

10 | CHAPTER 10
ADDING A REGISTRATION PAGE

RIGHT NOW OUR WEB APP, if launched, would let our users browse the items and objects we list but with no way for them to sign up for an account and to create their own objects. Shall we fix that?

Installing our first third party plugin

One of the best things about Django and its open-source community is the sheer number of plugins that developers created to make others' (and our) lives easier.

We're going to install a plugin called *django-registration-redux* (http://hellowebapp.com/23) that'll help us set up everything we need for user registration.

We're going to use pip to install. Make sure you're in your virtual environment, then type this into your command line:

```
$ pip install django-registration-redux==1.3
```

Next, you'll need to tell Django that we've installed this plugin—like we did when we added collection but this time

it's an external app we're installing. Head to *settings.py* and add
`registration` to the list:

```
INSTALLED_APPS = (
    'collection',
    'django.contrib.admin',
    'django.contrib.auth',
    'django.contrib.contenttypes',
    'django.contrib.sessions',
    'django.contrib.messages',
    'django.contrib.staticfiles',
    'django.contrib.humanize',
    'registration',
)
```

We'll also need to add more setting to our *settings.py* file,
according to django-registration-redux's documentation
(http://hellowebapp.com/24). Add this line at the bottom
of *settings.py*:

```
ACCOUNT_ACTIVATION_DAYS = 7
```

django-registration-redux will set up account activation
emails automatically for new users, and this required setting
lets us specify the number of days the user has to activate the
account before the ability to use the account expires. Let's
keep it at the default 7 for now.

Last, django-registration-redux comes with some migration
files that we need to apply to our database. Apply these using
`python manage.py migrate`:

```
$ python manage.py migrate
Operations to perform:
  Apply all migrations: sessions, admin, collection, content-
types, auth, registration
Running migrations:
```

```
Rendering model states... DONE
Applying registration.0001_initial... OK
Applying registration.0002_registrationprofile_activated... OK
Applying registration.0003_migrate_activatedstatus... OK
```

Setting up the URLs

We're going to basically import django-registration-redux's URLs for use in our app, which is fairly simple.

Head over to *urls.py* and add the lines indicated:

urls.py
```
# add to the top
from django.conf.urls import url, include


urlpatterns = [
    ...
    # new line we're adding!
    url(r'^accounts/', include('registration.backends.simple.urls')),
    url(r'^admin/', include(admin.site.urls)),
]
```

The new line basically says, "For any URL path starting with *accounts/*, search for a matching URL path in django-registration-redux's URLs."

Add "email" ability to your app

Django comes with the ability to send emails if you set up an email server, or you can just output the contents of the emails directly to your command line in a similar window to where `python manage.py runserver` is running. Let's set up the latter (we can add actual email functionality when we launch the app).

Head back to *settings.py* and add these lines to the bottom:

```
EMAIL_BACKEND = 'django.core.mail.backends.console.EmailBackend'
DEFAULT_FROM_EMAIL = 'testing@example.com'
EMAIL_HOST_USER = ''
EMAIL_HOST_PASSWORD = ''
EMAIL_USE_TLS = False
EMAIL_PORT = 1025
```

While we're here, let's tell Django what page we want to redirect to after successful registration. Add after the code block above:

```
LOGIN_REDIRECT_URL = "home"
```

Adding in the required templates

django-registration-redux also assumes that we have several templates already added to our app (More info: http://hellowebapp.com/25). We're going to create a new folder in our templates directory to hold these new templates:

```
$ cd collection/templates/
collection/templates $ mkdir registration
collection/templates $ cd registration
collection/templates/registration $ touch registration_form.html
```

Continue to use `touch` to create blank files in this directory with the following file names:

- *registration_form.html* (already created)
- *registration_complete.html*
- *login.html*
- *logout.html*

Thank goodness that the code inside of these templates will be fairly easy to create.

Start filling in our templates

The majority of code in these templates is just text or a form, which is created by Django. For the sake of brevity, I recommend the following content for each file:

login.html
```
{% extends 'base.html' %}
{% block title %}
    Login - {{ block.super }}
{% endblock title %}
{% block content %}
    <h1>Login</h1>
    <form role="form" action="" method="post">
        {% csrf_token %}
        {{ form.as_p }}
        <input type="submit" value="Submit" />
    </form>
{% endblock content %}
```

logout.html
```
{% extends 'base.html' %}
{% block title %}
    Logout - {{ block.super }}
{% endblock title %}
{% block content %}
    <h1>Logged Out</h1>
    <p>You have been logged out!</p>
{% endblock content %}
```

registration_complete.html
```
{% extends 'base.html' %}
{% block title %}
    Registration Complete - {{ block.super }}
{% endblock title %}
{% block content %}
    <h1>Registration Complete</h1>
```

```
    <p>Your account has been registered!</p>
{% endblock content %}
```

registration_form.html
```
{% extends 'base.html' %}
{% block title %}
    Registration Form - {{ block.super }}
{% endblock title %}
{% block content %}
    <h1>Registration Form</h1>
    <form role="form" action="" method="post">
        {% csrf_token %}
        {{ form.as_p }}
        <input type="submit" value="Submit" />
    </form>
{% endblock content %}
```

Add links to nav to login and logout

The last thing we should do is add a link to login and logout in our navigation. Update your *base.html* layout file:

base.html
```
    ...
    <ul>
        <li>
            <a href="{% url 'home' %}">Home</a>
        </li>
        <li>
            <a href="{% url 'about' %}">About</a>
        </li>
        <li>
            <a href="{% url 'contact' %}">Contact</a>
        </li>
        {% if user.is_authenticated %}
        <li>
            <a href="{% url 'auth_logout' %}">Logout</a>
```

```
        </li>
        {% else %}
        <li>
            <a href="{% url 'auth_login' %}">Login</a>
        </li>
        <li>
            <a href="{% url 'registration_register' %}">Register</a>
        </li>
        {% endif %}
    </ul>

    ...
```

Note the two extra links we're adding to the navigation.
`{% if user.is_authenticated %}` does what it looks like it
does—returns `True` if the current user is logged into your app.
Django by default automatically adds the current user for use
in templates.

Everything you need for someone to create an account and
login or logout should all be set up now. Open up your website
and check it out:

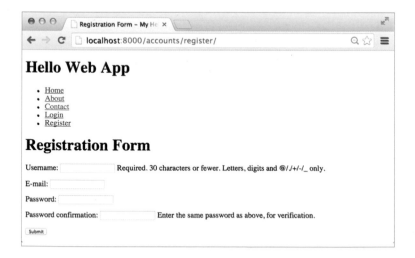

Try creating a couple new users.

Back into your admin (*http://localhost:8000/admin/*) you can see the new users created:

Unfortunately there's no way yet for our new users to start adding Things—users can only register, log in, and log out at the moment.

Setting up password reset functionality

Django comes with a lot of optional native password reset functionality that we just need to activate by setting up the appropriate URLs and templates.

Like earlier, here's the full list of templates to create in the registration directory:

- *password_change_done.html*

- *password_change_form.html*

- *password_reset_complete.html*

- *password_reset_confirm.html*

- *password_reset_done.html*

- *password_reset_email.txt*

- *password_reset_form.html*

And the content to put in the templates—quite a few files, but very simple content.

password_change_done.html
```
{% extends 'base.html' %}
{% block title %}
    Password Change Done - {{ block.super }}
{% endblock title %}

{% block content %}
    <h1>Password Change Done</h1>
    <p>Your password was changed.</p>
{% endblock content %}
```

password_change_form.html
```
{% extends 'base.html' %}
{% block title %}
    Password Change Form - {{ block.super }}
{% endblock title %}
{% block content %}
    <h1>Password Change Form</h1>
    <form role="form" action="" method="post">
        {% csrf_token %}
        {{ form.as_p }}
        <input type="submit" value="Submit" />
    </form>
{% endblock content %}
```

password_reset_complete.html
```
{% extends 'base.html' %}
{% block title %}
    Password Reset Complete - {{ block.super }}
{% endblock title %}
{% block content %}
```

```
    <h1>Password Reset Complete</h1>
    <p>Your password has been reset!</p>
{% endblock content %}
```

password_reset_confirm.html

```
{% extends 'base.html' %}
{% block title %}
    Confirm Password Reset - {{ block.super }}
{% endblock title %}
{% block content %}
    {% if validlink %}
    <h1>Confirm Password Reset</h1>
    <p>Please enter your new password twice so we can verify
        you typed it in correctly.</p>
    <form role="form" action="" method="post">
        {% csrf_token %}
        {{ form.as_p }}
        <input type="submit" value="Change password" />
    </form>
    {% else %}
    <h1>Password reset unsuccessful</h1>
    <p>The password reset link was invalid, possibly because
        it has already been used. Please request a new password
        reset.</p>
    {% endif %}
{% endblock content %}
```

password_reset_done.html

```
{% extends 'base.html' %}
{% block title %}
    Password Reset Done - {{ block.super }}
{% endblock title %}
{% block content %}
    <h1>Password Reset Complete</h1>
    <p>Check your email for a link to reset your password!</p>
{% endblock content %}
```

password_reset_email.txt

```
{% autoescape off %}
You're receiving this email because you requested a password
reset.

Please go to the following page and choose a new password:
{% block reset_link %}{{ protocol }}://localhost:8000{% url
'django.contrib.auth.views.password_reset_confirm' uidb64=uid
token=token %} {% endblock %}

Your username, in case you've forgotten: {{ user.username }}
{% endautoescape %}
```

password_reset_form.html

```
{% extends 'base.html' %}
{% block title %}
    Password Reset Form - {{ block.super }}
{% endblock title %}
{% block content %}
    <h1>Password Reset Form</h1>
    <form role="form" action="" method="post">
        {% csrf_token %}
        {{ form.as_p }}
        <input type="submit" value="Submit" />
    </form>
{% endblock content %}
```

Setting up the URLs

We'll need to tell Django we're using its password reset/
recover feature, so add these URLs to your *urls.py*:

urls.py

```
# add to our import statements at the top
from django.contrib.auth.views import (
    password_reset,
    password_reset_done,
```

```
        password_reset_confirm,
        password_reset_complete,
)

urlpatterns = [
    ...
    # the new password reset URLs
    url(r'^accounts/password/reset/$', password_reset,
        {'template_name': 'registration/password_reset_form.html'},
        name="password_reset"),
    url(r'^accounts/password/reset/done/$',
        password_reset_done,
        {'template_name': 'registration/password_reset_done.html'},
        name="password_reset_done"),
    # the below should all be on one line
    url(r'^accounts/password/reset/(?P<uidb64>[0-9A-
Za-z_\-]+)/(?P<token>[0-9A-Za-z]{1,13}-[0-9A-Za-z]{1,20})/$',
        password_reset_confirm,
        {'template_name': 'registration/password_reset_confirm.html'},
        name="password_reset_confirm"),
    url(r'^accounts/password/done/$',
        password_reset_complete,
        {'template_name': 'registration/password_reset_complete.html'},
        name="password_reset_complete"),
    url(r'^accounts/', include('registration.backends.simple.urls')),
    url(r'^admin/', include(admin.site.urls)),
]
```

Also, note that our import statement is wrapped in parentheses—when your imports get too long, add parentheses so the statement can span multiple lines. Otherwise, Python will throw an "unexpected indent" error.

We're overriding the default URL paths that come with Django so we can point to the template we created. Otherwise, Django will just point to the admin templates, which wouldn't match the style and layout of our web app.

Adding a link for password reset

Password change and password reset sound similar, but a change is for users who are already logged in, and reset is for users who can't log in because they forgot their password. Therefore, users should reset their passwords from the login page. Update your login template to the following:

login.html
```
{% extends 'base.html' %}
{% block title %}
    Login - {{ block.super }}
{% endblock title %}
{% block content %}
    <h1>Login</h1>
    <form role="form" action="" method="post">
        {% csrf_token %}
        {{ form.as_p }}
        <input type="submit" value="Submit" />
    </form>
    <p>
        <a href="{% url 'password_reset' %}">
            Forgot your password?
        </a>
    </p>
{% endblock content %}
```

Check out your website in the browser and play around with registering new "users," logging in, and logging out.

When you put in an email to reset the password for an account, check out your command line window to see your "email", which should look something like the below:

```
[27/Dec/2014 00:29:34] "GET /accounts/password/reset/ HTTP/1.1" 200 1079
MIME-Version: 1.0
Content-Type: text/plain; charset="utf-8"
```

```
Content-Transfer-Encoding: 7bit
Subject: Password reset on localhost:8000
From: testing@example.com
To: tracy+auser@weddinglovely.com
Date: Sat, 27 Dec 2014 00:29:47 -0000
Message-ID: <20141227002947.9192.76935@Orion.local>

You're receiving this email because you requested a password
reset for your user account at localhost:8000.

Please go to the following page and choose a new password:

http://localhost:8000/accounts/password/reset/Mg3xw-7ef-
c197726f67cb60e84/

Your username, in case you've forgotten: auser

Thanks for using our site!
The localhost:8000 team
```

Paste the link into your browser to complete the password
reset process:

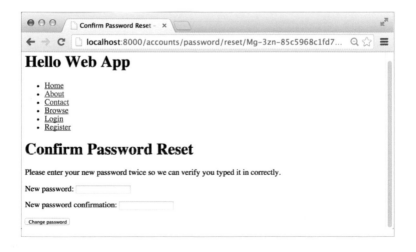

Hello Web App

- Home
- About
- Contact
- Browse
- Login
- Register

Password Reset Complete

Your password has been reset!

Now you see how password resetting functionality is built into Django and just needs a few templates created to access it.

Next chapter, we're going to tie these new users to objects in our database, so someone can create an account and a new object at the same time, as well as log in and update their object as well. Commit your work if you haven't already!

ASSOCIATING USERS WITH OBJECTS

THESE NEW "USERS" CAN'T CREATE AND UPDATE THINGS YET in our database. We're going to assume a one-to-one database relationship between users and Things—that is users can only create and update one Thing. This works best for schemes like "profiles in a directory" but less so for "items in a store." For the sake of brevity, we're going to stick with the former but will give some resources later in the book if you're building something where users will need to have multiple Things.

Changing our model so Users can own a Thing

First thing we need to do is tie our Thing model to our Users model, so every Thing is owned by one and only one User.

Update your Thing model (or whatever you called it) to the following:

models.py
```
# don't forget to import this
from django.contrib.auth.models import User
```

```
from django.db import models

class Thing(models.Model):
    name = models.CharField(max_length=255)
    description = models.TextField()
    slug = models.SlugField(unique=True)
    # the new line we're adding
    user = models.OneToOneField(User, blank=True, null=True)
```

We're in a tiny bit of a pickle. We're saying that each Thing
needs to have a unique User. Remember the migrations stuff
we did earlier? We'll need to migrate the database to this new
schema. Visualize a spreadsheet of Things with all their attributes—we need to add a new column for the Thing's User, and
fill that in for each row.

To make this easy, we're going to tell Django that it's okay
if the Thing doesn't have a User assigned to it—that's the
blank=True, null=True stuff we added. That way we don't
have to worry about filling in the previous objects created, just
our future ones.

Migrating your database

Create the migration by running the command below:

```
$ python manage.py makemigrations
Migrations for 'collection':
  0002_thing_user.py:
    - Add field user to thing
```

And then apply the migration:

```
$ python manage.py migrate
Operations to perform:
  Synchronize unmigrated apps: registration
  Apply all migrations: admin, contenttypes, collection, auth, sessions
```

```
Synchronizing apps without migrations:
  Creating tables...
  Installing custom SQL...
  Installing indexes...
Running migrations:
  Applying collection.0002_thing_user... OK
```

Now your Things can have a User owning them!

Updating your registration flow

You're almost done with this doozy of a chapter. The last thing
we need to do is set up an additional registration page so when
a new user signs up, they'll also set up their Thing.

Adding an additional form to our registration flow

We're going to set it up so after a user creates their username
and password, our web app will send them to an additional
form to create their Thing.

First, add a couple new URLs to our *urls.py* file:

```
# add this to the top
from collection.backends import MyRegistrationView

urlpatterns = [
    ...
    url(r'^accounts/register/$', MyRegistrationView.as_view(),
        name='registration_register'),
    url(r'^accounts/create_thing/$',
        views.create_thing,
        name='registration_create_thing'),
    url(r'^accounts/', include('registration.backends.default.urls')),
    url(r'^admin/', include(admin.site.urls)),
]
```

Then head back over to *views.py* to create the new view:

views.py

```python
# add at the top
from django.template.defaultfilters import slugify

# add below your edit_thing view
def create_thing(request):
    form_class = ThingForm
    # if we're coming from a submitted form, do this
    if request.method == 'POST':
        # grab the data from the submitted form and apply to
        # the form
        form = form_class(request.POST)
        if form.is_valid():
            # create an instance but do not save yet
            thing = form.save(commit=False)
            # set the additional details
            thing.user = request.user
            thing.slug = slugify(thing.name)
            # save the object
            thing.save()
            # redirect to our newly created thing
            return redirect('thing_detail', slug=thing.slug)
    # otherwise just create the form
    else:
        form = form_class()

    return render(request, 'things/create_thing.html', {
        'form': form,
    })
```

We're going to be reusing the form (ThingForm) we made before! Next, we'll need to create the template. Create the file:

```
$ cd collection/templates/things
collection/templates/things $ touch create_thing.html
```

Then fill it out:

create_thing.html
```
{% extends 'base.html' %}
{% block title %}
    Create a Thing - {{ block.super }}
{% endblock title %}

{% block content %}
    <h1>Create a Thing</h1>
    <form role="form" action="" method="post">
        {% csrf_token %}
        {{ form.as p }}
        <input type="submit" value="Submit" />
    </form>
{% endblock content %}
```

Very last thing we need to do is tell django-registration-redux to go to this form's page after successful registration instead of the registration complete page.

We're going to accomplish this by *subclassing* a portion of django-registration-redux. This is a powerful way to override bits of code in open-source plugins, so you can change only the bit you want to change, rather than rewriting the entire plugin.

We're going to put this piece of overwritten code in its own file. In your `collection` app, create a file called *backends.py*:

```
$ cd collection
collection $ touch backends.py
```

Here are the contents of the new *backends.py*:

backends.py

```
from registration.backends.simple.views import RegistrationView

# my new reg view, subclassing RegistrationView from our plugin
class MyRegistrationView(RegistrationView):
    def get_success_url(self, request, user):
        # the named URL that we want to redirect to after
        # successful registration
        return ('registration_create_thing')
```

How did we know about this? Check out django-registration-redux's documentation on views (**http://hellowebapp. com/26**)—this page lists out all the classes included in django-registration-redux and what is recommended to subclass. You can also browse all the code on the django-registration-redux GitHub repository (**http://hellowebapp.com/27**).

Check out your web app—users can now register for your website, which prompts them to create a Thing, and after successful registration, plops them into the newly created Thing page with a link to edit it.

Update permissions to edit objects

We probably want to make it so the owner of a Thing can edit only his or her respective Thing. Update your Thing template so the link is hidden to anyone who isn't logged in:

thing_detail.html

```
{% extends 'base.html' %}
{% block title %}
    {{ thing.name }} - {{ block.super }}
{% endblock title %}

{% block content %}
    <h1>{{ thing.name }}</h1>
    <p>{{ thing.description }}</p>
```

```
{% if user == thing.user %}
    <p>
        <a href="{% url 'edit_thing' slug=thing.slug %}">
            Edit me!
        </a>
    </p>
{% endif %}
{% endblock content %}
```

We also want to add some additional security precautions to
our view to make sure that we let non-owners edit information
that isn't theirs.

Update your *views.py:*

```
from django.contrib.auth.decorators import login_required
from django.http import Http404

...

@login_required
def edit_thing(request, slug):
    # grab the object...
    thing = Thing.objects.get(slug=slug)

    # make sure the logged in user is the owner of the thing
    if thing.user != request.user:
        raise Http404

    # set the form we're using...
    form_class = ThingForm

    # if we're coming to this view from a submitted form,
    # do this
    if request.method == 'POST':
        # grab the data from the submitted form and apply to
        # the form
        form = form_class(data=request.POST, instance=thing)
        if form.is_valid():
```

```
        # save the new data
        form.save()
        return redirect('thing_detail', slug=thing.slug)

    # otherwise just create the form
    else:
        form = form_class(instance=thing)

    # and render the template
    return render(request, 'things/edit_thing.html', {
        'thing': thing,
        'form': form,
    })
```

We're adding two important security measures—adding a *decorator* to our view (@login_required) that basically says, "The only people who can access this view are ones who are logged in." The second thing we're doing is checking the Thing we're grabbing the edit page for, and creating a 404 "Page not found" error if the logged-in user isn't the owner of the Thing. You, as admin, can still update/edit all info from your admin panel, but this prevents users from editing other users' information.

Our longest, most intense chapter yet! I hope this chapter gave you a better idea on how you can extend open-source plugins, update them to satisfy your needs, and how to keep data secure on your website.

One last thing — we set up the templates to do a password update for logged in users (that's the *password_change* templates we set up before). Can you figure out how to add that yourself?

Commit your work before moving forward!

12 | CHAPTER 12
SETTING UP BASIC BROWSE PAGES

RIGHT NOW OUR APP ALLOWS PEOPLE TO SIGN UP, create a Thing, and then edit their Thing. However, the only way for users to browse all the Things your web app contains is by going to your homepage. Let's set up a basic page to browse our items.

Note: *We won't be setting up text search, like Google, due to it being way more complex and beyond the scope of this book. If you're interested in learning more about how to do this, check out Haystack (*http://hellowebapp.com/28*).*

As we only have a few fields on our model, let's build a page that just lists every Thing we have by name.

You'll probably want to add browse pages for each of those fields as you fill out your model with new fields for what you're specifically building. For example, my first Django project had fields for price range and location, and therefore "narrow by price" and "narrow by location" pages. We're going to build a simple example here, which is easily copied for other use-cases.

Set up your URL routing

Back to the familiar URLs-views-templates routine. Add in
these new lines:

urls.py

```
. . .
urlpatterns = [
    . . .
    # our new browse flow
    url(r'^browse/name/$',
        views.browse_by_name, name='browse'),
    url(r'^browse/name/(?P<initial>[-\w]+)/$',
        views.browse_by_name, name='browse_by_name'),
    # password reset URLs
    url(r'^accounts/password/reset/$',
        password_reset,
        {'template_name': 'registration/password_reset_form.html'},
        name="password_reset"),
```

We're going to set up two new URLs at once: The first, which
we'll list out every Thing's name with a link to its page. The
second will allow us to specify a letter (*/browse/name/a/* to
search for names of Things that start with "a," for example.)

Set up the view

Next, off to your *views.py* to add this new view:

views.py

```
def browse_by_name(request, initial=None):
    if initial:
        things = Thing.objects.filter(
            name__istartswith=initial).order_by('name')
    else:
        things = Thing.objects.all().order_by('name')
```

```
return render(request, 'search/search.html', {
    'things': things,
    'initial': initial,
})
```

We created one view which works for both URLs. Neat, right?

The top line of the view where we have initial=None, this simply says that if there is no value passed in, then to assign it to None. So /browse/, which doesn't pass in initial letter, will have initial assigned to None. If you didn't have the None part, Python would whine that it expects something if it's empty.

Then we use an if-statement to determine what kind of database query we want to do, depending on whether we are passing something in or not.

We're also using name__istartswith, another queryset filter like contains which we used before (More info: http://hellowebapp.com/29). Note that we don't *have* to use a single letter to search—this code will work whether you searched for 'a' or 'hello', grabbing everything in your database that starts with your query.

Fairly simple, and making one view rather than two means less code, ergo less maintenance.

Create the template

Last, our template. We're going to create one "search" template that'll work for both flows here and we can extend in the future for other browse cases.

Create a new directory for search in your templates, and then create your *search.html* file:

```
$ cd collection/templates/
collection/templates $ mkdir search
collection/templates $ cd search
collection/templates/search $ touch search.html
```

Note: *Technically we're browsing, not searching, but I find calling the pages and process "search" easier.*

Our *search.html* file:

```
{% extends 'base.html' %}
{% block title %}
    Browse - {{ block.super }}
{% endblock title %}

{% block content %}
    <h1>
        Browse Things{% if initial %} Starting with
        '{{ initial|title }}'{% endif %}
    </h1>

    {% for letter in 'abcdefghijklmnopqrstuvwxyz' %}
    <a href="{% url 'browse_by_name' initial=letter %}"
        {% if initial == letter %}class="active"{% endif %}>
        {{ letter|upper }}
    </a>
    {% endfor %}

    <ul>
        {% for thing in things %}
        <li><a href="{% url 'thing_detail' slug=thing.slug %}">
            {{ thing.name }}
        </a></li>
        {% empty %}
        <li>Sorry, no results!</li>
        {% endfor %}
    </ul>
{% endblock content %}
```

We're doing quite a few fun things here.

- First, our headline. We're modifying the headline depending whether "initial" exists or not. Users will get a descriptive headline for both cases.

- Note that in the headline, we have `initial|title`—one of the template tags we talked about earlier in Chapter 4. Why not `|upper`? I mentioned before this actually works with any letter or word, and chose `|title` so, if we searched for "hello" it would be displayed as "Hello" rather than "HELLO."

- To display links for every letter in the alphabet, we're looping over the alphabet in the template. Again, less code (as compared to writing out all the links) means less maintenance.

- We're adding an `active` class to the currently selected letter, which you can style using CSS.

- We're looping over the lowercase alphabet but making it uppercase when displayed. This way our links look like /browse/name/a/ rather than /browse/name/A/. Both work, but the former looks better.

- We loop over every result in our list and display a link to the `Thing`.

- Last, `{% empty %}` is what the for loop will display if the list we pass in is empty.

Updating your nav and setting up redirects

There isn't a link to this page in the main nav, so we should update the nav:

base.html
```
...
<li>
    <a href="{% url 'contact' %}">Contact</a>
</li>
<li>
    <a href="{% url 'browse' %}">Browse</a>
</li>
```

The second nitpick is our URL—*/browse/name/* works, as well as */browse/name/a/...* but */browse/* will 404 since we haven't set up a route for it. It's not linked to, but someone might edit the URL in their browser. Let's redirect */browse/* page to */browse/name/* (adding `permanent` makes it a 301 redirect, rather than 302).

Updated *urls.py*:
```
# added RedirectView to this import statement
from django.views.generic import TemplateView, RedirectView

    ...
    # our new redirect view
    url(r'^browse/$', RedirectView.as_view(
        pattern_name='browse', permanent=True)),
    url(r'^browse/name/$',
        views.browse_by_name, name='browse'),
```

```
url(r'^browse/name/(?P<initial>[-\w]+)/$',
    views.browse_by_name, name='browse_by_name'),
```

Like `TemplateView`, which we used before to display a template without writing a view (for our *About* and *Contact* pages), `RedirectView` is another generic view that let's us avoid writing extra code and sets up a simple redirect.

We have another set of URLs that could benefit from this same treatment. Let's redirect */things/* to our browse page as well:

urls.py

```
    . . .
    url(r'^things/$', RedirectView.as_view(
        pattern_name='browse', permanent=True)),
    url(r'^things/(?P<slug>[-\w]+)/$',
        views.thing_detail, name='thing_detail'),
    url(r'^things/(?P<slug>[-\w]+)/edit/$',
        views.edit_thing, name='edit_thing'),
    . . .
```

Test the redirects out by going to *http://localhost:8000/browse/* and *http://localhost:8000/things/* and watch them automatically redirect to the correct pages.

There we go, a great start to building browsable pages for your website visitors. Commit your work!

13 | CHAPTER 13
QUICK HITS: 404 PAGES, REQUIREMENTS.TXT, AND TESTING

WE'RE GOING TO GO OVER SOME SMALL THINGS in this chapter that aren't worthy of pulling out into a chapter of their own. Simple things that are pretty important.

Setting up 404 and 500 error pages

When you're going through this tutorial, because you're working locally and your DEBUG setting in *settings.py* is set to True, Django gives you a nice error page with all the info about your error. However, it's not good to show that info to random users of your web app.

Head to *settings.py* and change DEBUG to `False`. Additionally, Django will whine unless we update the ALLOWED_HOSTS setting. Right now, let's set it to everything (A.K.A., we'll allow any host), but add a note that we should update it to our future domain on our launched app for security's sake.

```
DEBUG = False
# XXX: Update me before launch!
ALLOWED_HOSTS = ['*']
```

Check out what happens when you go to a non-existent page and get a 404 response:

Ew, a default browser page not using our app's styles. Let's add a 404 page, shall we?

Add your template files

Create *404.html* and *500.html* files in your templates directory:

```
$ cd collection/templates/
collection/templates $ touch 404.html
collection/templates $ touch 500.html
```

Then update the template contents:

404.html
```
{% extends 'base.html' %}
{% block title %}
    404 - {{ block.super }}
{% endblock title %}

{% block content %}
    <h1>404 Error</h1>
```

```
    <p>You've run into a page that doesn't exist!</p>
{% endblock content %}
```

500.html
```
{% extends 'base.html' %}
{% block title %}
    500 - {{ block.super }}
{% endblock title %}

{% block content %}
    <h1>500 Error</h1>
    <p>You've run into an error!</p>
{% endblock content %}
```

That's all you need to do! Take a look at the broken page again in your browser:

Custom error pages, woohoo! Make sure to change DEBUG in *settings.py* back to True before you move on.

Setting up a requirements.txt

This part of the chapter won't make any website changes or be visible to your future users, but will make setting up your app on other computers and working with others much easier.

A *requirements.txt* file lists everything installed in your virtual environment for your project. If you ever had a clean virtual environment in the future and needed to install everything to make your web app work, you could run `pip install -r requirements.txt` and pip will go through the entire list and install everything at once. It's a convention for Python, and super useful.

First, let's get a list of everything installed so far. Run `pip freeze` in your command line (make sure you're in your virtual environment first):

```
$ pip freeze
Django==1.9.1
django-registration-redux==1.3
wsgiref==0.1.2
```

We installed the first two, and the last (`wsgiref`) is something installed by virtualenv. To set up your *requirements.txt*, make sure you're in the top level directory (the same one as *manage.py*) and pipe the contents of `pip freeze` into the new file:

```
$ pip freeze > requirements.txt
```

Check out your new *requirements.txt* file, which should look like the below:

requirements.txt
```
Django==1.9.1
django-registration-redux==1.3
wsgiref==0.1.2
```

That's all you need to do. You can test it out by running `pip install -r requirements.txt`, and pip will let you know everything is installed already:

```
$ pip install -r requirements.txt
Requirement already satisfied (use --upgrade to upgrade):
Django==1.9.1 in ./venv/lib/python2.7/site-packages (from -r
requirements.txt (line 1))
Requirement already satisfied (use --upgrade to upgrade):
django-registration-redux==1.3 in ./venv/lib/python2.7/
site-packages (from -r requirements.txt (line 2))
Requirement already satisfied (use --upgrade to upgrade):
wsgiref==0.1.2 in /usr/local/Cellar/python/2.7.8_1/Frameworks/
Python.framework/Versions/2.7/lib/python2.7 (from -r require-
ments.txt (line 3))
Cleaning up...
```

Awesome. Future you or friends can install your app more easily now by installing from your requirements file!

Setting up your first tests

When you have your app deployed live to the world, nothing is worse than making a "quick change," deploying, and then discovering you broke a major feature or (worse) took down the entire site. This is especially common when your app does a lot of different things that tie together in ways that you might forget—change one thing and something else breaks. You could manually go through the website yourself, making sure everything works by clicking from page to page and testing features, but that's time consuming.

That's why we write tests, so we can run a command and test our functionality in the command line, making sure the site is up and everything works without having to test manually.

Let's set up a basic test to make sure our site is working without errors. Django created a file already for your tests in your collection app. Update it to the below:

tests.py

```python
from django.test import TestCase

class CollectionTest(TestCase):
    def test_index(self):
        r = self.client.get('/')
        self.assertEqual(r.status_code, 200)

    def test_no_logic_page(self):
        r = self.client.get('/about/')
        self.assertEqual(r.status_code, 200)
```

We're creating tests for our `collection` app, first testing whether our homepage pops up, and then testing whether a simple no-logic page (our "about" page) works as well. For each, we're "grabbing" the page and assigning it to the variable r, and then asserting whether the page's status code equals 200 (which, as you know, means OK. More info: http://hellowebapp.com/30)

To run the test, head back to your command line and run `python manage.py test`, and you should see the below output:

```
$ python manage.py test
Creating test database for alias 'default'…
..
Ran 2 tests in 0.033s
OK Destroying test database for alias 'default'...
```

Boom, ran 2 tests, and everything was OK.

What if something went wrong? Go into your *views.py* and add a typo to your index view:

```python
def index(request):
    things = Thing.objects.all()
    return render(request, 'index.html', {
```

```
    # typo below!
    'things': thinggs,
})
```

And then run your tests again:

```
$ python manage.py test
Creating test database for alias 'default'...
E.
ERROR: test_index (collection.tests.CollectionTest)
Traceback (most recent call last): File "/Users/limedaring/
projects/testhwa/collection/tests.py", line 9, in test_index
r = self.client.get('/')
  ...
  File "/Users/limedaring/projects/testhwa/collection/views.
py", line 14, in index
  'things': thinggs,
NameError: global name 'thinggs' is not defined

Ran 2 tests in 0.044s
FAILED (errors=1) Destroying test database for alias
'default'...
```

Nifty, right? Make sure to fix the typo and commit your work.
Read more about Django tests here: http://hellowebapp.com/31

Get into the practice of running your tests often, and especially
before deploying your web app live. Might save your bacon!

14
DEPLOYING YOUR WEB APP

IT'S REALLY IMPORTANT FOR YOU TO KNOW how to push your web app onto the internet so anyone in the world can access it—unfortunately, this is also one of the most difficult parts of web app development. I'm going to walk you through the steps in order to launch your website on Heroku, which is the easiest-to-use hosting solution, but the steps here are still going to be slightly complicated. Stick with it, it'll be worth it. If you get stuck, head to the *Hello Web App* discussion forum for help: http://discuss.hellowebapp.com

In order to use Heroku, we'll need to install some extra utilities and set up some extra files. After everything is set up, you can continue to develop locally and deploy new versions of your web app live with ease.

Note: *On Windows and something isn't working? Check out the discussion forums mentioned above for troubleshooting since Windows and Heroku sometimes don't play nicely together.*

Setting up Heroku

You'll first need to create a free account with Heroku (http://hellowebapp.com/32), and eventually end up at your dashboard:

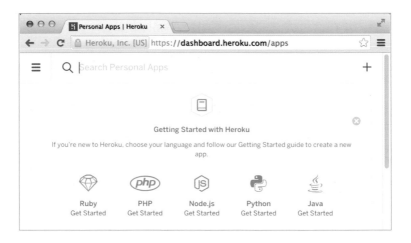

Click on the Python button, and Heroku will prompt you to install the Heroku Toolbelt (http://hellowebapp.com/33), which lets you log in to Heroku and run other Heroku commands from your command line. The next page of instructions will instruct you to clone an existing project to learn deployment—ignore these and just move on below.

Setting up a public key

If you try to log in to Heroku from your command line and get the error, `Permission denied (publickey)` we'll need to set up your public/private key. This is a security measure to uniquely identify you as the developer of this web app, so Heroku can make sure only you are the one pushing code changes.

If you already have a public/private key pair set up, feel free to move onto the next section.

In your command line, generate the public key by running this command:

```
$ ssh-keygen -t rsa
```

The default file location in which to save the key is fine, just press enter at the prompt. Second, it'll ask for a passphrase—choose something secure that you'll remember. The final output should look something like this:

```
$ ssh-keygen -t rsa
Generating public/private rsa key pair.
Enter file in which to save the key (/Users/limedaring/.ssh/id_rsa):
Enter passphrase (empty for no passphrase):
Enter same passphrase again:
Your identification has been saved in /Users/limedaring/.ssh/id_rsa.
Your public key has been saved in /Users/limedaring/.ssh/id_rsa.pub.
The key fingerprint is:
a6:88:0a:0b:74:90:c6:e9:d5:49:d6:e3:04:d5:6c:3e limedaring@
workstation.local
```

Once you log in again using `heroku login` in your command line, Heroku should find and upload your private key automatically.

Installing a few extra packages

We'll need to install a few other packages required by Heroku. Make sure you're in your virtual environment, then run `pip install hellowebapp-deploy` in your command line. This will install:

- *waitress:* A web server for Python apps.

- *dj-database-url:* A Django configuration helper.

- *whitenoise:* Allows you to serve static files in production.

In the previous chapter, we created a *requirements.txt* file. Now that we've installed new packages, make sure to update it. Rather than piping `pip freeze` over, we're just going to open up and add `hellowebapp-deploy` to the list like below:

requirements.txt

```
Django==1.9.1
django-registration-redux==1.3
wsgiref==0.1.2
hellowebapp-deploy
```

We're not adding a version number, so pip will install the latest version when we install our requirements. Also, why not `pip freeze > requirements.txt`? Run `pip freeze` in your command line, and you should see something like below:

```
$ pip freeze
Django==1.9.1
dj-database-url==0.3.0
django-registration-redux==1.3
waitress==0.8.10
hellowebapp-deploy==1.0.2
whitenoise==2.0.6
wsgiref==0.1.2
```

`hellowebapp-deploy` installs the rest of those packages, no need to clutter up our *requirements.txt* file with the extra installs.

There's one last thing we're going to add to our *requirements.txt* file, that we're **not** going to install: `psycopg2`. Heroku's database will be *PostgreSQL* (more on this below), and Heroku will be using our *requirements.txt* to know what to install on our server. `psycopg2` is a PostgreSQL adapter for Python, required by Heroku. Locally though, we're using SQLite3 for our database, because it's 100x easier to set up than PostgreSQL for beginners. If we installed `psycopg2` locally, it would throw an error because PostgreSQL isn't installed on your system. So we're going to add it to our *requirements.txt* so Heroku installs it, but not install it locally.

New *requirements.txt*:
```
Django==1.8.4
django-registration-redux==1.2
wsgiref==0.1.2
hellowebapp-deploy
psycopg2==2.6.1
```

Creating your Procfile

A *Procfile* is something Heroku defined to let users run all kinds of different applications on their platform. Way back when, you could only run Ruby applications on Heroku, but thanks to the Procfile you can run your Django application there too (More info: http://hellowebapp.com/34).

Let's make a Procfile in our top level directory (the one with *manage.py*) to tell Heroku how to run our app:

```
$ touch Procfile
```

And update it to the below:

Procfile
```
web: waitress-serve --port=$PORT hellowebapp.wsgi:application
```

This tells Heroku that we want to run a process under the "web" category using waitress, the Python web server we installed earlier.

Setting up your static files for production

Django serves your static files up in a working, but inefficient manner when you're developing on your computer. Because of its inefficiency and likely vulnerabilities, we need to take a couple of different steps to get static files working in production on our live website. One of the packages we installed above, whitenoise, will help us out here. We just need to configure a few things.

Update the *wsgi.py* file that was automatically created when we made our Django project way back in the day to the below:

wsgi.py
```
import os
os.environ.setdefault("DJANGO_SETTINGS_MODULE",
    "hellowebapp.settings")

from django.core.wsgi import get_wsgi_application
from whitenoise.django import DjangoWhiteNoise

application = get_wsgi_application()
application = DjangoWhiteNoise(application)
```

We then need to update *settings.py* for whitenoise. Add these two new settings below STATIC_URL:

settings.py
```
STATIC_URL = '/static/'
STATIC_ROOT = 'staticfiles'
STATICFILES_DIRS = (
    os.path.join(BASE_DIR, 'static'),
)
```

There's one last silly thing we need to do to set up static files on Heroku. Heroku will automatically run the command collectstatic on your app, which collect **all** static files into one folder. However, this process will fail if we don't give it an empty folder to store these files in.

In the same folder as *manage.py*, create a new directory named "static" and add an empty file to it:

```
$ mkdir static
$ cd static
static $ touch robots.txt
```

(I'm adding *robots.txt* just because you might need it later on, and it's fine being blank for now.)

Creating your app on Heroku

Let's tell Heroku this is the project we want to deploy. Run this in your command line:

```
$ heroku create
```

This will create a "space" for your app in your Heroku account.

Heroku uses git to push our code, so make sure everything is committed at this point:

```
$ git commit -a -m "Committing before pushing to Heroku."
```

Let's push our code to Heroku, which you can do by running this command:

```
$ git push heroku master
```

You're going to see a lot of processes fly by—Heroku installing the packages you've installed like Django and hellowebapp-deploy, moving over your static files, and starting the server.

Last, add a web process to your app, which Heroku calls "dynos." Basically, this tells Heroku to actually start serving your website:

```
$ heroku ps:scale web=1
```

We're not quite ready to launch the website—the last thing we need to do is set up our database.

Setting up your production database

Way back in the day when we created our local database, we made a SQLite database, which is the easiest to create, but not good for production on your live server.

Reminder: SQLite3 databases are perfect for small single-user applications, like ones that run on your computer and only you're using them. Web browsers such as Safari use SQLite to store and query all kinds of data. They're not stable when many people try to use your application at once, like when it's served on the public Internet.

We're going to set up a separate settings file that'll be used only in Heroku. That way we can specify a production-ready database (as mentioned before, PostgreSQL). This is also useful if you ever work with something that has "test" and "live" API keys, so you can put your test API key in your local settings file and put your live key in your production settings file (for example, working with Stripe for payments).

In the same folder as *settings.py*, create *settings_production.py*:

```
$ cd hellowebapp
hellowebapp $ touch settings_production.py
```

And insert the following information:

settings_production.py
```
# Inherit from standard settings file for default
from hellowebapp.settings import *

# Everything below will override our standard settings:
# Parse database configuration from $DATABASE_URL
import dj_database_url
```

```
DATABASES['default'] = dj_database_url.config()

# Honor the 'X-Forwarded-Proto' header for request.is_secure()
SECURE_PROXY_SSL_HEADER = ('HTTP_X_FORWARDED_PROTO', 'https')

# Allow all host headers
ALLOWED_HOSTS = ['*']

# Set debug to False
DEBUG = False

# Static asset configuration
STATICFILES_STORAGE = 'whitenoise.django.GzipManifestStaticFilesStorage'
```

We're basically copy and pasting directly from Heroku's documentation on how to create a PostgreSQL database (More info: http://hellowebapp.com/35).

We also need to tell Heroku to use this settings file instead. Paste this into your command line (make sure you're in the same folder as *manage.py*):

```
$ heroku config:set DJANGO_SETTINGS_MODULE=hellowebapp.settings_production
```

As well as update your *wsgi.py* file:

```
...
os.environ.setdefault("DJANGO_SETTINGS_MODULE",
    "hellowebapp.settings_production")
```

Add the file to git, commit, and push your changes to Heroku:

```
$ git add .
$ git commit -a -m "Added production settings file."
$ git push heroku master
```

Run your migrations on your production server

Here's where you'll start to see why we do database migrations—we can easily apply all the changes we made locally by running migrate on the server:

```
$ heroku run python manage.py migrate
```

Last, we need to create a superuser again on the live server, like we did for our local server:

```
$ heroku run python manage.py createsuperuser
```

Your app should be ready! Run heroku open to pop it open in your browser.

Feel free to give your Heroku app a new name (rather than the random one Heroku gives you) by running the below command (replace YOURAPPNAME with a unique name for your app.)

```
$ heroku apps:rename YOURAPPNAME
```

Congrats, you've launched your web app!

For the future, as you develop locally, run the below steps to push it live:

- Commit your changes to git when you're ready to deploy.

- Run git push heroku master to push the changes to Heroku.

- Also worth it to run git push origin master if you've set up a remote GitHub repository to back your app up in the cloud.

WHAT TO DO IF YOUR APP IS BROKEN

YOU'LL PROBABLY SPEND MORE TIME trying to fix random errors than you will building your app. You might have heard jokes of programmers spending all night trying to fix an error only to find out that they were missing a simple comma. So if you run into an error, you're not alone—debugging happens to the best of us. If you're stuck, here's some ideas to help you debug your app.

Error pages *usually* help you find the problem

Generally the error page you get when developing locally will tell you what and where the problem is. Here, I have a syntax error on line 13 in my *views.py* file.

The offending line:

```
return render(request, 'search/search.html' {
```

Nothing obvious on first glance, but it really should be:

```
return render(request, 'search/search.html', {
```

Missing comma! Those pesky things. Easy to fix once you find it, though.

What do you do if your error page isn't so helpful?

Googling the error usually comes up with helpful answers

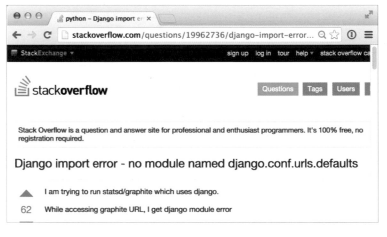

Copy/paste the error into Google and chances are, someone else had the same error and it's already answered—usally on Stack Overflow (http://hellowebapp.com/36), which is an immensely helpful website that people use to ask and answer programming questions.

Ask for help

You might have scanned your code inch by inch looking for the issue, and Googling isn't helping. What now?

IRC

IRC is essentially chat, with "rooms" that can be based around a topic, like Django. It's a little complicated to get going and might seem intimidating, but generally the strangers and future friends on IRC are happy to help others who are having problems.

If you already know how to use IRC, here are a couple channels on freenode to ask questions:

* `#django`
* `#python`
* `##learnpython`
* `#pyladies`

(Of course, make sure to be polite and specific as possible when explaining your problem.)

New to IRC? Check out our IRC page on the *Hello Web App* GitHub page here with instructions: http://hellowebapp.com/37

Stack Overflow

Obviously, you can also ask for help on Stack Overflow. Just like IRC, make sure to be as descriptive as possible when explaining your issue. Here's a link to ask a question on Stack Overflow: http://hellowebapp.com/38.

Mailing lists

There is a django-users mailing list (http://hellowebapp.com/39) where people ask questions and help each other. If you're not in a rush, this could be a good place to write up your problem and get some feedback on how to proceed.

Before posting, it's good form to search through the archive (http://hellowebapp.com/40) to see if somebody asked a similar question yet. This will also help you get a feel for the format that most messages are in.

Meetups and developer events

Need face to face help? There are hundreds of meetups and developer events worldwide, and there is likely one in the city near you. Here are some great organizations that run meetups and places to find meetups:

- PyLadies (http://hellowebapp.com/41)

- Python meetups on Meetup.com (http://hellowebapp.com/42)

- Django Girls (http://hellowebapp.com/43)

You can also search for "Python meetup YOURCITY" to see if there is something happening near you.

These events are also a great place to meet new friends and expand your programming community!

16 | CHAPTER 16
IMPORTANT THINGS TO KNOW

THERE ARE A FEW THINGS AND PRINCIPLES you should know about building web apps. Generally you can do whatever you want (have fun programming!) but keep these points in mind:

Code style

Python has a style guide known as PEP 8 which gives coding conventions and gives recommendations—such as, the numbers of space per indent (four), comment styling (above the code, starting with # and a single space), and other tidbits.

Why is this important? These conventions will keep your code consistent and readable, to yourself in the future as well as for any others who will read your code.

The style guide includes recommendations like this:

```
Yes: spam(ham[1], {eggs: 2})
No:  spam( ham[ 1 ], { eggs: 2 } )
```

Read more about PEP 8 and the Python style guide here:
http://hellowebapp.com/44

Documentation

Another recommendation for your future self as well as other reviewers of your code—good documentation.

This might seem superfluous while you're programing—of course you know what's going on as you're typing it—but you could come back later and think, "What the heck was I doing?"

It's always a good idea to add comments above your code to describe what's going on. For example, random chuck of code from my startup's app:

```python
for line in fileinput.input(paths):
    if not line.strip():
        # Empty line
        continue

    # Split the log into its' individual parts
    access = parse_access_log(line)
    if not access:
        continue

    user_agent = access['user_agent']
    if "bot" in user_agent:
        # ignore everything with "bot" in the name
        continue

    # Check if we're in the desired parsing range. If not, skip
    # or exit.
    if time_since and timestamp < time_since:
        # Fast forward
        continue
    else:
        # None specified, assume from the first entry.
        time_since, time_until = timestamp_to_range(timestamp)
```

```
if time_until and timestamp >= time_until:
    # Done
    return time_until
```

You could write the above without the comments, but it's a lot easier to read and skim with them added. It's always a good idea to document what you're doing as you go.

More on this topic: http://hellowebapp.com/45

Security

I remember when I was building my first web app and I showed it to a friend before launch. He immediately went to the page where users could update their logic and figured out that the number in my edit page URL (*http://mywebapp.com/edit/1*) corresponded to the ID of the object, so he could change it to something like /21/ and see another person's object, and then edit it because I wasn't checking for ownership when displaying the page. Duh, right? It stands out to me as the first time I realized that people were going to try to actively break my app, and that I needed to always keep in mind security precautions

Back in "Adding a Registration Page," we added the @login_required decorator as well as checking ownership on the object when updating the edit page to make sure you don't make the same mistakes I did.

Another issue I had with my app back in the day was a silly favoriting ability I added: users could save their favorites as they browsed the site. I didn't require the users to have an account—I saved the favorite with their session_id in the database. However, months later I discovered that there seemed to be a bot going through all of my listings and favoriting everything, causing hundreds of database saves and drastically slowing down (and sometimes taking down) my site. Seriously? Someone did that to me?

That problem has since been fixed, but again, my tiny little site got targeted by people looking to break it. Keep an eye out for vulnerabilities that your app could have and try to prevent things like this. For more about potential security issues you could run into, check out this article:
http://hellowebapp.com/46

Using the Django shell

When I first started learning how to program, I felt more comfortable building my views and seeing the results in the template—and I suspect a lot of other beginners are the same, thus the format of this book. Most experienced programmers don't do this, however, preferring to test code in the command line window. It's faster, once you get used to it.

Like how we ran `python manage.py runserver` in the command line (feel free to open a new window if you'd like), run `python manage.py shell`:

```
$ python manage.py shell
Python 2.7.8 (default, Aug 24 2014, 21:26:19)
[GCC 4.2.1 Compatible Apple LLVM 5.1 (clang-503.0.40)] on darwin
Type "help", "copyright", "credits" or "license" for more
information.
(InteractiveConsole)
>>>
```

Here, you can import settings and run commands just like in your *views.py*, but see instantaneous results.

```
>>> from collection.models import Thing
>>> things = Thing.objects.all()
>>> for thing in things:
...     print thing
...
Hello Thing
```

```
Another Thing
Yet Another!
Another Name of a Thing
```

The first three lines were commands I typed in — first import-ing `Thing` from our models, then running a query to grab all of our `Thing`s, then running a for-loop to print all of the `Thing` names. When the shell detects a code block (like our for loop), it'll give you another row to type the next line in (make sure to add the indent.) An extra return will indicate that you're done with the command. This is hard to explain in print—try it out and play around and it should become more clear.

When you create more complex views, you can walk through the code in your shell to confirm that it's working correctly before seeing the results in the template. You can also use it to grab and update information in your database without using the admin panel (but make sure to be careful so you don't erase or overwrite information that you need.)

In a nut shell, the shell is a handy skill to have once you're comfortable using it.

17 | CHAPTER 17
MOVING FORWARD

YOU'VE CREATED YOUR FIRST WEB APP using *Hello Web App*—congratulations! I'm proud of you. I hope that I've ignited the spark to learn more (and hopefully gotten you on the path to building the next billion dollar company, perhaps.)

Now what? Here are some resources and advice to continue your education.

Keep building your app

When I started my first app, I got better at programming in general by improving my app and adding new features. For example, learning how to monetize the app by integrating Stripe and PayPal, creating new search pages, creating administration pages, etc. Each of these additional features started with me thinking, "Huh, I wonder how to add payments from customers," and led to a rabbit hole of Googling for help, playing around with ideas, testing, and eventually launching the new feature. Don't be scared of learning while doing—it's a great way to teach yourself.

Great books and additional reading

Hello Web App intentionally glossed over a lot of programming details to show you how fast you can get started with web app development. The below resources will help you start filling in your knowledge.

Hello Web App: Intermediate Concepts by Tracy Osborn:
http://hellowebapp.com/intermediate-concepts
Hey, that author looks familiar! *Intermediate Concepts* is the official follow up to this book, covering more complex features such as adding payments and user-uploaded images as well as intermediate concepts like proper database design. Use HWAREADER in the purchase form for 10% off.

Two Scoops of Django by Audrey Roy Greenfield and Daniel Greenfield: http://hellowebapp.com/47
Two Scoops is a resource book for Django best practices and expands on pretty much everything mentioned here. I definitely recommend adding this to your reading list.

Test-Driven Development with Python by Harry J. W. Percival: http://hellowebapp.com/48
Interested in learning more about tests? The ones we did back in Chapter 13 are pretty much the very bare minimum—here, you'll learn how to build tests first before writing your main code.

Additional tutorials and resources

There are quite a few tutorials ranging from beginner to intermediate that you can jump into to walk through expanding your app.

Django Girls Tutorial: http://hellowebapp.com/49
Very comprehensive beginner tutorial for Django, not just for girls.

Django's official polls tutorial: http://hellowebapp.com/50
Cement your knowledge by going over an additional beginner
course provided by the Django Software Foundation. Again,
Hello Web App glossed over some aspects of programming that
this tutorial will go over a bit more in depth.

Django Packages: http://hellowebapp.com/51
Great directory listing reusable Django apps, packages, and
tools that you can use for your own app.

Free online classes

If you love the format of learning in a school-like environment,
there are a lot of online courses you can take to learn more.
Here are a few of my favorites:

Codecademy: http://hellowebapp.com/52
Courses on HTML, CSS, Javascript, jQuery, Python, Ruby, and
PHP, all interactive and free.

Coursera: http://hellowebapp.com/53
Coursera lists a lot of great programming courses—Python,
Django, programming in general, marketing, and more.

More resources can be found here: http://hellowebapp.com/54

In-person programming schools and development courses

There are many, many schools and in-person courses that
you can take to take your development skills to the next level.
Below is a short list of my favorites—more can be found by a
quick internet search.

Hackbright Academy - San Francisco, CA:
http://hellowebapp.com/55
Hackbright Academy is a programming fellowship created for women in San Francisco. I've heard a lot of great things about this program—a fast-track course to becoming a full-fledged software engineer. Requires an application. Tuition is $15,000 and there are scholarships available.

The Recurse Center—New York City, NY:
http://hellowebapp.com/56
Less specific tutorials and programming help and more of a "retreat" to explore programming on your own with the support of your fellows. The Recurse Center also helps connect their members with jobs if that's something you're looking for. Each round is three months and requires an application. The Recurse Center is free, and has grants to cover living expenses in NYC for minorities.

Ladies Learning Code—Many cities, Canada:
http://hellowebapp.com/57
Ladies Learning Code is a not-for-profit organization dedicated to helping women and kids learn to code. They have chapters and run workshops in many cities in Canada. Workshops generally cost a small amount—for example, $50 CAD for a half-day course.

RocketU Full-Stack Developer Bootcamp—
San Francisco, CA: http://hellowebapp.com/58
A 12-week intensive bootcamp teaching full-stack development in San Francisco. Requires application and costs $12,500.

General Assembly's classes—In person (many locations) and online: http://hellowebapp.com/59
A lot of great general programming courses and other educational lessons. Topics range from design to development, and course lengths range from full-time, part-time, and one-day offerings.

Stay in touch with *Hello Web App*

Last but not least, I encourage you to stay in touch with this book's online resources. If you haven't already, check out http://hellowebapp.com and sign up for the email newsletter. I'll be sending updates about this book, new resources, as well as announcing new editions and books in the *Hello* series—there is a good chance *Hello Web Design* will be next!

As mentioned earlier in the book, we also have a discussion forum, and I'd love to see what you've built using this book: http://discuss.hellowebapp.com

I also would love to chat with you on Twitter: http://twitter.com/hellowebapp (official book account) or http://twitter.com/limedaring (personal).

Keep in touch, and best of luck building your web apps!

SPECIAL THANKS

This book couldn't have been written without the support of my friends, family, and Kickstarter backers (friends from afar!)

Super thanks to our sponsor

The biggest thanks goes to Kinsights (http://kinsights.com) for sponsoring *Hello Web App* on Kickstarter, and in particular for pushing the campaign over its goal. A bit about them:

> *Kinsights is a free advice-sharing network for parents. Get advice from parents that you'll actually use. Learning Django? Join a group of other Django-loving parents here:*
> https://kinsights.com/for/django

Book reviewers, editors, and testers

I tested (and tested, and tested) this book and yet things still snuck through. The hugest thanks to those that took the time to review, edit, and run all the code bits contained within this book—your feedback was invaluable.

Andrey Petrov
Kenneth Love
Carol Willing
Drew Gerlach
Glen Gilchrist
Hans Meldgaard
Kerstin Kollmann
Leland Richardson

Matthew Oliphant
Olya Sanakoev
Osvaldo Santana Neto
Peter Westlake
Richard Cornish
Siow Chen Ang
Vincent Smith

Help and suggestions

I wouldn't have made it this far without having a lot of smart people giving suggestions and lending help.

Julia Elman
Michael Trythall
Kenneth Love
Audrey Roy Greenfield

Daniel Greenfield
Jonathan Snook
Poornima Vijayashanker

Kickstarter backers

Hello Web App's Kickstarter campaign was a success due to the generosity of the folks below. Again, my sincere thanks:

Aidan Nulman
Alejandro Krumkamp
Andreas Djunaedi
Andrew Louis
Andrew Wasem
Andy Giffen
Angie Chang
Ben Blumenfeld
Bryan Veloso
Carol Naslund Willing
Chris Spicer
Cory Benfield
Daly Chang
David Ritter
Ed Stockman
Ellen Amudipe
Enrique Piedrafita
Frederic Tschannen
Jackie Ta Jannis Leidel
Jeremy Gillick
Julio Carlos Menéndez

González
Kara Beyer
Kathleen Tuite
M. Jackson Wilkinson
Maria khomenko
Marta Maria Casetti
Martin Kleppmann
Matthew Oliphant
Noah Kantrowitz
Olivier Yiptong
Ozzie Sabina
Rachel Cordray Sanders
Ryan Feeley
Sam Stokes
Samuel Clay
Theodore Tedwardson III
Thomas A Kent
Tim Kuehlhorn
Toby Bettridge
Turki Alotieschan
Tzu-ping Chung

REFERENCES

For reference, the shortened link URLs throughout the book and their related long URL are listed below.

Chapter 2

1 http://amzn.to/1qUIE8o
2 http://learn.shayhowe.com/html-css/
3 http://www.dontfeartheinternet.com/
4 http://learnpythonthehardway.org/
5 http://pyvideo.org/video/2559/hands-on-intro-to-python-for-beginning-programmer
6 https://github.com/limedaring/HelloWebApp/tree/master/python-tips
7 https://github.com/hellowebapp/hellowebapp/tree/master/windows-help

Chapter 3

8 https://github.com/limedaring/HelloWebApp/tree/master/installation-instructions
9 https://github.com/limedaring/HelloWebApp-Code
10 httpxs://discuss.hellowebapp.com
11 https://github.com/limedaring/HelloWebApp

Chapter 4

12 https://github.com/limedaring/HelloWebApp/tree/master/git-tips

Chapter 5

13 http://learnpythonthehardway.org/book/ex29.html
14 https://docs.djangoproject.com/en/1.7/ref/templates/builtins/

15 https://docs.djangoproject.com/en/1.7/ref/contrib/humanize/

Chapter 6

16 https://github.com/limedaring/HelloWebApp/blob/master/
installation-instructions/starting-your-project.md
17 https://docs.djangoproject.com/en/dev/ref/models/fields/#slug-
field

Chapter 7

18 https://docs.djangoproject.com/en/1.7/ref/models/querysets/

Chapter 8

19 https://docs.python.org/2/howto/regex.html

Chapter 9

20 https://docs.djangoproject.com/en/dev/topics/forms/model-
forms
21 https://docs.djangoproject.com/en/dev/ref/csrf/
22 https://docs.djangoproject.com/en/dev/topics/forms/#form-ren-
dering-options

Chapter 10

23 https://django-registration-redux.readthedocs.org
24 https://django-registration-redux.readthedocs.org/en/latest/
quickstart.html#settings
25 https://django-registration-redux.readthedocs.org/en/latest/
quickstart.html#required-templates
26 http://django-registration-redux.readthedocs.org/en/stable/
views.html
27 https://github.com/macropin/django-registration/

Chapter 11

28 http://haystacksearch.org/
29 https://docs.djangoproject.com/en/dev/ref/models/query-sets/#istartswith

Chapter 12

30 http://www.w3.org/Protocols/rfc2616/rfc2616-sec10.html
31 https://docs.djangoproject.com/en/1.7/topics/testing/overview/

Chapter 13

32 http://heroku.com
33 https://devcenter.heroku.com/articles/getting-started-with-python#set-up
34 https://devcenter.heroku.com/articles/procfile
35 https://devcenter.heroku.com/articles/getting-started-with-django#django-settings

Chapter 14

36 http://stackoverflow.com/
37 https://github.com/limedaring/HelloWebApp/tree/master/irc-tips
38 https://stackoverflow.com/users/login?returnurl=%2fquestions%2fask
39 https://docs.djangoproject.com/en/1.7/internals/mailing-lists/#django-users
40 https://groups.google.com/forum/#!forum/django-users
41 http://www.pyladies.com/
42 http://python.meetup.com/
43 http://djangogirls.org

Chapter 15

44 https://www.python.org/dev/peps/pep-0008/
45 http://docs.writethedocs.org/writing/beginners-guide-to-docs/

46 http://www.djangobook.com/en/2.0/chapter20.html

Chapter 16

47 http://amzn.to/13sLUh6
48 http://amzn.to/1GrwlUF
49 http://tutorial.djangogirls.org/en/
50 https://docs.djangoproject.com/en/dev/intro/tutorial01/
51 https://www.djangopackages.com/
52 http://www.codecademy.com/
53 https://www.coursera.org/courses?query=python
54 https://github.com/limedaring/HelloWebApp/tree/master/additional-resources
55 http://www.hackbrightacademy.com/
56 https://www.hackerschool.com/
57 http://ladieslearningcode.com/
58 http://rocket-space.com/rocketu/
59 https://generalassemb.ly/education/

INDEX

COLOPHON

The text is set in Tisa Pro with Tisa Sans Pro for sub-headlines both by FontFont. Chapter headlines are set in Alternate Gothic No. 3 D by URW++. Code is set in Inconsolata by Raph Levien. Cover and page footers are set in Avenir by Adrian Frutiger.

FRIENDLY NOTE

Hello Web App is entirely self-published by Tracy Osborn and is purposely DRM-free. If you've come across this book for free and enjoyed it, I invite you to make a donation at http://hellowebapp.com/donate. Your support is appreciated!

ABOUT THE AUTHOR

Tracy Osborn is a designer, developer, and entrepreneur living in the Bay Area of California. Building websites since she was twelve, she always felt an affinity to computers, the internet, and what it brings us.

Tracy graduated with a BFA in Art & Design with a concentration in Graphic Design from California Polytechnic State University, San Luis Obispo, and worked as a web designer for five years before teaching herself programming and launching her first startup, WeddingLovely.

She's also an avid outdoorswoman, hiking over 200 miles on the John Muir Trail solo in 2014.